Anywaa

Anywaa

The Luo of Western Ethiopia

JEKAP OMOD
Foreword by Doug McGill

RESOURCE *Publications* · Eugene, Oregon

ANYWAA
The Luo of Western Ethiopia

Copyright © 2024 Jekap Omod. All rights reserved. Except for brief quotations in critical publications or reviews, no part of this book may be reproduced in any manner without prior written permission from the publisher. Write: Permissions, Wipf and Stock Publishers, 199 W. 8th Ave., Suite 3, Eugene, OR 97401.

Resource Publications
An Imprint of Wipf and Stock Publishers
199 W. 8th Ave., Suite 3
Eugene, OR 97401

www.wipfandstock.com

PAPERBACK ISBN: 979-8-3852-1817-2
HARDCOVER ISBN: 979-8-3852-1818-9
EBOOK ISBN: 979-8-3852-1819-6

08/06/24

Contents

Lists of Illustrations and Tables — vii
Foreword by Doug McGill — ix
Preface — xiii
Acknowledgments — xv
Abbreviations — xvii
Introduction — xix

Part 1

Chapter 1	The Anywaa Relationship with Murle and Nuer People	3
Chapter 2	The Anywaa Country and British Colonial	13
Chapter 3	Slavery under Imperial Ethiopia	24
Chapter 4	American Missionaries to the Anywaa People	32

Part 2

Chapter 5	Anywaa under the Communist Derg Regime	41
Chapter 6	The Refugees in Anywaa Lands	50
Chapter 7	The Birth of the GPLM Party	58
Chapter 8	The Downfall of the GPLM Party	70

Part 3

| Chapter 9 | The Anywaa Genocide | 79 |
| Chapter 10 | The Crimes against Humanity | 93 |

Contents

Chapter 11	Revenge against the EPRDF	99
Chapter 12	The Anywaa People Post-Genocide	108
Chapter 13	Living under the Oppression	116

Part 4

Chapter 14	Dhal-diim	127
Chapter 15	Lwaa-Ceri	141
Chapter 16	The OLA/F-Shene and GLF attack on Gambella	149
Chapter 17	Institutionalized Colorism against Dark-Skinned Gambellans	154

Glossary	167
Interviewees	173
References	175

Lists of Illustrations and Tables

Figure 1	12
Figure 2	45
Figure 3	49
Figure 4	69
Figure 5	92
Figure 6	98
Figure 7	107
Figure 8	138
Figure 9	139
Figure 10	140
Figure 11	140
Figure 12	140
Figure 13	148

Foreword

OVER THE PAST CENTURY, more than 600 of humanity's unique indigenous cultures have become extinct, vanishing forever from the world.

Today, one human language disappears every two weeks. As each of these indigenous cultures vanishes, its storehouse of traditional wisdom, laws and rituals, healing practices, music, art and language is extinguished from humanity's life.

The gripping drama of the Anywaa tribe of Ethiopia illuminates one indigenous culture's slide towards extinction. Through painstaking documentation, care to establish historical context, and achingly graphic stories of the Anywaa's encounter with modernity, this book sounds an ominous warning. It reminds us of all that's lost when ancient human cultures are ground to dust.

The Anywaa today are vastly diminished, but not yet extinct. That gives ground for hope although the tribe's survival, if it does survive, will be in a drastically weakened and reduced form.

A century ago, the Anywaa population in Ethiopia and Sudan numbered more than 350,000. Today, fewer than 100,000 Anywaa remain. The sources of the Anywaa's decline are many, but in recent times distills down to one: Ethiopia's policy of ethnic cleansing against them. Intermittent massacres conducted by Ethiopian military and police over many decades, plus more recent policies of forced-resettlement of the Anywaa, have killed thousands, and driven thousands more to flee as refugees. Today, more Anywaa live across a global diaspora in the U.S., Canada, Australia and Europe, than live in Ethiopia.

The Anywaa's story represents, in microcosm, virtually the same plight faced by 5,000 endangered indigenous cultures, encompassing 450 million people, in 90 countries worldwide.

Foreword

The Anywaa's homeland is richly fertile, being fed by several rivers, and is also rich in gold deposits. Their land is thus ideal for exploitation by large-scale agriculture and mining projects, another common thread in the worldwide oppression of indigenous cultures. Clearing the Anywaa from their lands, by whatever means necessary, has been a linchpin of Ethiopia's long-term plan to seize and offer that land for sale to investors eager to build lucrative commercial projects.

Living remote from civilization for decades, the Anywaa have been defenseless against the Ethiopian military, who have carried out their ethnic cleansing policy openly, without fear of exposure. With brutal regularity, Anywaa villages have been burned to the ground, and thousands of Anywaa massacred by gunshot in broad daylight.

A single day—December 13, 2003—marks the bloodiest massacre in the Anywaa's history. On this day, according to Human Rights Watch and Genocide Watch, more than 420 Anywaa were slaughtered, many of their women raped, and hundreds of homes were torched by uniformed Ethiopian soldiers and police. As they moved from home to home in Gambella, the Anywaa's largest town, the soldiers held a typed list of 750 men marked for execution. As the men were found, they were seized from their homes, summarily shot, and their corpses left on the streets. Eyewitness survivors recalled how soldiers, as they gang-raped Anywaa women, shouted how this act would dilute the tribe's blood.

In this book, the ordeals of the Anywaa are firmly placed in the roll-call of indigenous cultures that met similar fates: the Tutsis of Rwanda; the Fur, Basalit and Saghawa tribes of Darfur; the Maya of Guatemala; the East Timorese of Indonesia; the Muslims of Bosnia; the Kurds of Iraq; the Armenians of Turkey; the Aborigines of Australia; the native Indians of the United States; and others.

The Anywaa's story also offers a lens through which to grasp the complex weave of historical, economic, social, cultural and human factors that bring indigenous cultures to the edge of extinction, or tip them over. As an example, the Anywaa's ancestral lands in Ethiopia reach into Sudan, and border clashes between the two countries figure large in this account. In the 19th-century, those battles were fought on Anywaa land as the Abyssinian Empire (later known as Ethiopia) and Sudan's 20th-century colonial ruler, the United Kingdom, fought to define and control the border between the two nations. Today, the Anywaa land is still a zone of conflict, only now pitting the tiny tribe against the modern Ethiopian state.

Foreword

As well, modern-day Ethiopia has used the tribe's longstanding frictions with neighboring tribes, especially the Nuer of Sudan and Ethiopia, as a weapon against the Anywaa. Traditionally, Anywaa-Nuer tensions played out in low-intensity, low-fatality skirmishes over grazing lands for cattle. By arming the Nuer with rifles, Ethiopia escalated these minor conflicts into full-scale massacres of the Anywaa, who bore only spears.

Today, the ethnic cleansing of the Anywaa continues, not only through brute military force, but by the government's policy of forced resettlement, euphemized as "villagization." In this way, Anywaa are swept away by seizing their homes and busing them to barren locations, to clear their lands for commercial projects.

A Swiss anthropologist, Conradin Perner, studied and lived for years in Anywaa villages, indeed, for long enough to be formally given an Anywaa name, Kwacakworo. In the Anywaa tongue, the name means "leopard," connoting a courageous and clever person who readily adapts to challenging environments.

Following his fieldwork, Perner/Kwacakworo published a series of lushly-illustrated ethnographies of the Anywaa society and culture, called "Living on Earth in the Sky." The eight-volume series describes the richness of indigenous Anywaa traditions including its myths, kinship and social structures, political system, language, art, dance, music, natural healing methods, laws and guidelines for sustainable farming and hunting, and traditional practices for resolving conflicts peacefully.

"Despite the external pressures, the Anywaa have shown remarkable resilience," Perner/Kwacakworo writes. "Their stubborn belief in the essential goodness of existence and the positive forces of life has helped them preserve their cultural identity."

In these pages, against all odds, the Anywaa's belief in the positive force of its ancient culture is once again proclaimed, and lives on.

Doug McGill

Preface

GROWING UP IN GAMBELLA, Ethiopia, during the era of the Tigray People's Liberation Front (TPLF) government, I came to question many things that I was taught in school, learned in the community, or heard about the Anywaa people when I went to places outside of Gambella such as Addis Ababa. In searching for information about the history of the Anywaa people, I realized that most of the histories about them were written by the British, Americans, and a few Ethiopian highlanders. None of them were written by an Anywaa author from the perspective of the Anywaa people. In other words, the histories about the Anywaa people were not written by them, and that created misinterpretation and a vague history of the Anywaa. When I became active on social media such as Facebook and X (previously called Twitter), I came to realize that most Ethiopians have a totally different perspective about the history of the Anywaa people and Gambella region in general. As a dark-skinned Ethiopian and someone who grew up in Gambella, Ethiopia, I came across discrimination, colorism, and even racist name-calling by my fellow Ethiopians. This motivated me to dig down and learn about where all these negative perspectives originated from throughout the history of Gambella within the Ethiopian state.

Before coming to the United States in 2014, my family and I lived in Addis Ababa for three years. That was when I faced discrimination and colorism almost daily every time I went out or went to school. It became a norm to be called monkey, charcoal, *bariya* (meaning slave), *lamma*, or *shanqella*. Experiencing such hatred made me eager to investigate the history of Ethiopia with regards to the Nilotic or dark-skinned Ethiopians. As a genocide survivor and someone who witnessed a great displacement and land grabbing that took place in Gambella, I questioned whether the Anywaa people are really considered humans in Ethiopia. When I was at the University of Minnesota studying neuroscience, I was able to visit

Ethiopia in 2018, 2020, and 2021. I also visited after I finished school in 2022 and 2023. During my travels, I have faced the same racism and discrimination in Addis Ababa. Furthermore, I found that the Anywaa people still live under the same economic inequality, political oppression, and social discrimination in Gambella, despite the change of the government of Ethiopia. Therefore, I decided to write this book, capturing the previous and current situation of the Anywaa people which placed them at the verge of extinction.

Anywaa: The Luo of Western Ethiopia is written based on extensive research, personal experiences, in-person and phone interviews with eyewitnesses, and records of historical events throughout the history of the Anywaa people. During my research, I found similarities and differences of some historical events recorded by different writers about the Anywaa people. Through personal interviews with the Anywaa people in Gambella and Minnesota, I was able to point out and tell the stories through the perspective of the Anywaa people. As someone who is from the Anywaa community, I addressed the misconceptions and misrepresentations of the community. Even though the book covers some heart-wrenching adversities that the Anywaa community have endured throughout their history under the Ethiopia state and British colonial rule, I have discovered a great perseverance and persistence among the indigenous Anywaa people. In conclusion, *Anywaa: The Luo of Western Ethiopia* also serves as a call for justice, accountability, healing, and reconciliation.

Jekap Omod

Acknowledgments

THIS BOOK WOULDN'T HAVE been possible without the help and support from people in my Anywaa community. First, I want to thank reporter Agwa Gilo for connecting me with people that I wanted to interview. Secondly, I am very grateful for Commander Ngeeli Oliru and Commander Bare Agid for taking the time to meet with me despite their busy schedules. I couldn't thank them enough for briefly answering my questions and sharing their experiences with me. I thank them for all the sacrifices they made for the Anywaa people and the Anywaa lands; their works will be remembered for generations to come. I want to thank the former president of Gambella, Mr. Okello Akway, for opening up with me and sharing all the things he knows and witnessed during the Anywaa genocide. This book wouldn't be possible without his contribution and all the information he provided. I am thankful for two amazing elders in the Anywaa community in the United States: Mr. Oron Ochala and Mr. Willie Gilo Lumson. I want to thank them for sharing Anywaa history and the history of the GPLM Party with me. I am grateful for the knowledge and experiences that they shared with me about Gambella and the Anywaa people during the Derg and the TPLF government. I also want to thank Dr. Magn Ochala Cham (PhD) for giving me the time and talking to me about the Dhal-diim organization. I am grateful for sharing his knowledge and experiences with me about the Dhal-diim movement. I want to thank Mr. Awinya Nyigelo Ojaay for being vulnerable and sharing the history of the massacre that took place in Gambella Prison. Even though this was a traumatic event that personally affected his life, Mr. Awinya openly shared his experience with me.

Last but not least, I want to thank my family for supporting me throughout the process. I want to thank my father, Pastor Ojulu Oboya, for all the support he gave me throughout my education journey. I wouldn't be able to have the knowledge I have today without the sacrifice that my

Acknowledgments

father made by going beyond and even hiring a tutor for me when I first started school even though he was poor. Thank you, father, for giving me something that you didn't have: the opportunity to have an education. I also want to thank my mother, Okonyjwok Olwoch Othow, for being the backbone of the family. You sacrificed everything to raise us and everyone in the family. You are the strongest and the smartest mother I know. There wouldn't be a Jekap Omod or this book without a mother like you. Thank you for the sacrifices you made to get us where we are today. My degrees, books, and everything I have accomplished or will accomplish in the future are yours and belong to you. I also want to thank my siblings for being the best siblings on earth. Thank you for being supportive. And of course, I wouldn't end without thanking my partner and supporter, Debora Oboya Omod. Thank you, my love, for always giving me great advice, encouragement, and support. I am thankful to have a supportive partner like you in my life.

Abbreviations

ACANA	Anywaa Community Association in North America
ARRA	Administration for Refugee and Returnee Affairs
DBE	Development Bank of Ethiopia
E.C	Ethiopian Calendar
EEC	European Economic Commission
EDHS	Ethiopia Demographic and Health Surveys
EHRC	Ethiopian Human Rights Commission
ENDF	Ethiopian National Defense Force
EPLF	Eritrean People's Liberation Front
EPRDF	Ethiopian People's Revolutionary Democratic Front
EZEMA	Ethiopian Citizens for Social Justice
GLF	Gambella Liberation Front
GPDC	Gambella People's Democratic Congress
GPDF	Gambella People's Democratic Front
GPDUP	Gambella People's Democratic Unity Party
GPLM	Gambella People Liberation Movement
GPLP	Gambella People's Liberation Party
HRW	Human Rights Watch
ICIJ	International Consortium of Investigative Journalists
ID	Identity Document
NATO	North Atlantic Treaty Organization

Abbreviations

NIF	National Islamic Front
NGOs	Non-Governmental Organizations
OLF/A	Oromo Liberation Front/Army
PM	Prime Minister
POW	Prisoner of War
PP	Prosperity Party
RRS	Refugees and Returnees Services
SMNE	Solidarity Movement for a New Ethiopia
SPLM/A	Sudan People's Liberation Movement/Army
TPLF	Tigray People Liberation Front
UN	United Nations
UNHCR	United Nations High Commissioner for Refugees

Introduction

THE ANCESTRAL LANDS OF the Anywaa people—rich in waterways, fertile soil, agriculture, and minerals including gold—have been a blessing and a curse to the Anywaa. In modern times they have been a source of great trial and suffering, genocide, and the near-extinction of the Anywaa.

Historically, the Anywaa have lived in villages on both sides of the border separating southwest Ethiopia and southeastern Sudan. This fateful geography has in modern history placed the Anywaa at ground zero of many bloody military and guerrilla struggles waged within and between British Colonial Sudan to the west of Anywaa territory and Imperial Ethiopia to its east. Also, these great conflicts have vastly inflamed ancient hostilities between the Anywaa and neighboring tribes and ethnic groups including, but by no means limited to, the Nuer and Murle tribes of South Sudan and the Oromo of Ethiopia.

In the early twenty-first century, these many longstanding conflicts compounded each other exponentially, driving the Anywaa ever-closer to extinction.

Anywaa derives from *nywaak*, meaning "sharing," historically the supreme social value of the Anywaa. Over the years, the name *Anywaa* has been rendered in many ways, including *Anuak* by British colonists, and *Anywua*, *Anyuwaa*, and *Anyuak*, the latter the preferred spelling of the Swiss anthropologist, Conradin Perner, whose ethnographic studies of the Anywaa are definitive references.

Other northern African tribes and ethnic peoples live in lands directly adjacent to the Anywaa. To the east, the Gaala (Oromo) and the Cushitic-speaking Illubabor, and the Wollega people to the north. *Keewa kidi*, an Anywaa saying for "the mountain is the border," demarcates the limit of Anywaa lands to the south, where Oromo and Illubabor territory begins, and its limits to the north, separating the Anywaa from Oromo and Wollega

Introduction

peoples. To the south and west, the Anywaa share borders with the Murle and Nuer people.

Ethnically, the Anywaa belong to the far larger Luo Nilothic group, scattered throughout East and Central Africa, including the countries of South Sudan, Ethiopia, Kenya, Uganda, Tanzania, Congo, and Chad. Besides the Anywaa, the larger Luo includes the Collo (Shilluk), Acholi, Alur, Lango, Pari, Balanda, Boor, Luwo (Jur Chol), Thuri, Bwodho, Kumam, Jo-Padhola, Jo-Pawir, and Jo-Luo peoples, among others.

This book describes the efforts of the Anywaa people to maintain their cultural identity, and their very existence as a living culture, amidst a host of violent challenges in the early twentieth century. These challenges include frequent clashes with neighboring tribes, as well as periodic episodes of ethnic cleansing carried out by the police and national military of the nation of Ethiopia and with various guerrilla forces.

The modern period of the Anywaa kingdom, it can be said, began in 1882, when British colonial forces overthrew the government of Egypt in Cairo. The British then proceeded to occupy large swaths of Egypt and Sudan. To accomplish the occupation of southeastern Sudan, including roughly half of the total territory of the Anywaa kingdom, the British made alliances with the two greatest tribal enemies of the Anywaa, the Nuer and Murle tribes. Using weapons supplied to them by the British, the Nuer and Murle for decades have staged raids and massacres of Anywaa villages. Pressure from nomadic Arab tribes in South Sudan also forced ethnic Nuer, longtime enemies of the Anywaa, eastward into traditional Anywaa territory, deep into Sudan and Ethiopia, resulting in frequent clashes and displacement of Anywaa. During the twentieth-century expansion of Imperial Ethiopia, the Anywaa people were forced on many occasions to fight the Abyssinian empire to maintain their existence, autonomy, and identity as a living culture.

Living on fertile lands came with a great price to pay for the Anywaa people, making them a target of both Imperial Ethiopia and the British. Both powers sought control of Gambella,[1] the capital of southwest Ethiopia covering Anywaa land, thus leaving the Anywaa people no choice but to resist. Under Ethiopian rule, the Anywaa fought multiple wars to defend their kingdoms against the Abyssinian Empire, which often kidnapped Anywaa

---

1. Gambella is an Anywaa word combining two roots: *gam*, meaning "catch," and *bella*, meaning "tiger." The Anywaa people also use *bella* to signify sorghum, a staple food of the Anywaa.

INTRODUCTION

children, and forced heavy taxation. Meanwhile the British, from their base in Sudan, sought to colonize and oppress the Anywaa in the western portions of Anywaa land.

Many of these conflicts were fought for control of the many rivers running through Anywaa territory, numbering no less than seven: the Openo, Gilo, Alworo, Akobo, Oboth, Agwenymals, and Dikony rivers. Among these, the Openo River,[2] as crucial hub of trade in the region and crucial for navigation, was preeminent.

In 1902, during the reign of King Menelik II of Ethiopia, the Anywaa kingdom's territory was divided between the Abyssinian and British empires. The Sudanese government instantly regretted the demarcation and opened a trading post in Gambella on the right bank of Openo. The port was opened after the British asked King Menelik II to post a British officer in Gambella to administer the Anywaa territories, as Imperial Ethiopia had failed to do so. Subsequently, the port of Gambella, on the Openo River, became a major trading center, being used by British colonials from Sudan, and by Ethiopia, well into the 1990s. The first postal service was then opened in Gambella in 1915 by the British.

Slavery was legal in Imperial Ethiopia until Emperor Haile Selassie abolished it under pressure from Noel Buxton, a prominent British colonial administrator of the time. During this time, Gambella became a major trading center for slaves. Slave raiders of the Abyssinian empire fell especially upon the Opwo, Komo, and Majang people. Their lack of government structure, while living defenseless in geographically scattered villages, made these tribes more vulnerable than the Anywaa.

After the division of the Anywaa land, the Anywaa under Imperial Ethiopia continued to be underserved and marginalized. During this period, American missionaries provided the Anywaa with education and healthcare. The missionaries, with the permission of emperor Haile Selassie, taught the Anywaa people in their native language. In addition, the

---

2. The Openo River is the only navigable river in Ethiopia and has the second largest bridge in the country. The river was used as a port by Imperial Ethiopia, from which they exported coffee and ivory and received salt, clothes, and other goods. Like the Gilo River, another major waterway used by the Anywaa, the Openo is named after the Anywaa king. The name Openo River is also known as the Baro River, from the Oromo language, according to Kurimoto ("Multidimensional Impact"). The name *Baro*, derived from the Amharic word *bariya*, means "slave" and was bestowed by King Menelik II to connote a derogatory meaning of the Baro River as "the river of slaves" or "the river of black people."

INTRODUCTION

missionaries translated and published the Bible, using an anglicized language of the Anywaa, Dha-Anywaa, using an anglicized alphabet.

When King Haile Selassie was overthrown in 1974 by the Derg regime, a socialist government, the Anywaa kingdom was decimated. During the Derg regime, from 1974 to 1987, the Anywaa's traditional enemies, the Nuer, were allowed to advanced deep into the Anywaa lands in and around Gambella and to gain political power over the Anywaa.

The First Sudanese Civil War (1955–72) brought a massive influx of refugees to Anywaa territory around Gambella in Ethiopia. This book describes the impact of this flood of refugees on the Anywaa people, as well as the long-term demographic changes that started then and continue to this day. Also, the Derg brought thousands of Ethiopian settlers, known as "highlanders," into Gambella, drastically changing Gambella's demographics in Ethiopia's favor. This book also describes the creation of the Gambella Peoples' Liberation Movement (GPLM), an armed resistance group of Anywaa, formed in 1979, and the heightened tensions between the Anywaa and the Ethiopian government, led then by Prime Minister Meles Zenawi. Those mounting tensions exploded tragically for the Anywaa on December 13, 2003, when Ethiopian soldiers conducted a massive ethnic cleansing of Anywaa in Gambella, killing some 425 people, according to Human Rights Watch and other independent observers. Many of those killed were the male leaders of the Anywaa in Gambella, whose names were later found on lists carried by the marauding Ethiopian soldiers. This book describes in detail the role played in these conflicts by the Tigray People Liberation Front (TPLF) in the fall of GPLM, further weakening the Anywaa people.

In the years following the genocide of the Anywaa in December 2013, the surviving Anywaa of Gambella were subjected to years of continuing ambushes and killings, rapes, displacements of families, long incarcerations of Anywaa, land-grabbing of fertile agricultural tracts, and other forms of suppression that continue to this day. Altogether, the Anywaa believe that more than 6,000 people have been killed by the Ethiopian National Defense Force.

PART 1

Chapter 1

The Anywaa Relationship with Murle and Nuer People

THE MURLE AND NUER people are known by the Anywaa people as their traditional enemies. The relationship between these two tribes and the Anywaa people is historically mixed with tribal conflicts and encroachment. The Murle or Ajiibe[1] are a small ethnic group living in South Sudan's Jonglei State, south of the Anywaa's land. They are known for kidnapping children from the other ethnic groups that live around them such as Anywaa, Bor Dinka, and Lou Nuer. During dry seasons, Murle people usually cross the border to the Anywaa lands in Ethiopia and Southern Sudan and commit atrocities against the Anywaa community. They abduct children, kill mothers and fathers, steal cattle and weapons and cause much destruction to property. This has been going on for decades, and the Anywaa people had to always prepare and get ready when the dry seasons approached. The Anywaa defended themselves and protected their lands from the Murle's illegal activities for decades. Though the Murle people practiced stealing cattle, kidnapping, and killing for years, they're not interested in taking over the Anywaa's lands. But when it comes to the Nuer people, on top of stealing, killing, and kidnapping children, they also assimilate the people and take over the lands. Perner said:

---

1. *Ajiibe* is the Anywaa name for Murle; the singular word for Ajiibe is Ajiba.

> The Anyuak prefer Murle, even praise their bravery, probably because the Murle, in great contrast to the Nuer, have never taken physical possession of the Anuak territory.[2]

The Anywaa people defended their lands in Ethiopia against the Nuer and Murle threats for decades. However, the disarmament that took place during the Derg and TPLF government had left the Anywaa more vulnerable to attacks by the Murle people. Both the Derg regime and TPLF government were unable to protect Anywaa civilians, but they played a bigger role in demolishing the means of protection by disarming the Anywaa people, thus opening the door wide open for the Murle criminals to freely roam around and cross the border and commit atrocities on the defenseless Anywaa without any response. Dry seasons have become weeping seasons for the mothers, as this season became a time when Murle kidnap children and commit atrocities on Anywaa civilians. The lack of response by the governments of Ethiopia have caused many lives and much damage in Anywaa land. The first responsibility of any country is to protect its citizens. But this responsibility is not fulfilled when it comes to the Anywaa people in both Ethiopia and South Sudan. One of the things that the government of Ethiopia seems to use as an excuse is the massive border between Gambella and South Sudan.

The Nuer people also have their own goal of occupying Anywaa lands and creating their own country called "The Greater Naath Nation."[3] The first Anywaa lands occupied by the Nuer were Nyium Amiel (Nasir) and Akobo. The Nuer emigrated out from their land, Bentiu, and went to occupy the Anywaa lands of Nyium and Akobo. In his book, Perner stated:

> When people said that they were going to see (the) "nazir," they in fact meant the administrator residing there ("Nazir" means "administrator"). Indeed the place was known, at least to the Anyuak, as Nyium Amiel, referring to the Anyuak chief who had settled there ... When, in 1907, ten years after Dr. Junker's visit, a hunting expedition was organized by an "American gentleman living in Britain," W. N. McMillian arrived on the upper course of the Sobat. The Nuer had apparently already been occupying Nasir; the Anyuak, the former owners of the land of Nasir, were not there anymore.[4]

2. Perner, *Why Did You Come If You Leave Again*, 91.

3. The map of the Greater Naath Country included Gambella as one of the states. The Greater Nuer or Naath Country was planned out by the radical Nuer politicians who wanted to form an independent Nuer country that was not a part of South Sudan.

4. Perner, *Why Did You Come If You Leave Again*, 87–88.

The Anywaa Relationship with Murle and Nuer People

Nyium (Nasir) is one of the first Anywaa lands that the Nuer successfully occupied, and they forced the Anywaa people out of the land. One of the main reasons that forced Nuer people to invade Anywaa land was the Arabs' expansion. The oppression of the Arabs forced the Nuer to move toward the Anywaa land in the east. Opap[5] stated that a larger population of Nuer moved to the east in 1850 due to the Baqqara Arabs' oppression and slavery. Later, more Nuer migrated to the east as the Arabs' aggression increased. The Northern Sudanese are predominantly Arabs and Muslims that control the government, while Southern Sudan is occupied mostly by dark-skinned Africans (Nilotic), most of whom were Christians and pagans who had no power in the government. These differences led to oppression by the northern Arabs, forcing Islam on the southerners. The missionaries who were Christianizing the southerners were labeled enemies of the state by the Sudanese government, and the Nuer and other southerners faced persecution as they were also suspected of rebellions. The other cause of Nuer emigration to Anywaa lands was a search for green grass during dry seasons. As pastoralists, the Nuer people emigrate to wherever they see green grass and water. That is how they moved out from Nuer land to the Anywaa land of Akobo following the abundant green grass by the banks of Akobo River during dry seasons. The Anywaa people are mostly farmers, and they historically depended on farming the lands. They also meet their protein diet needs from fishing and hunting. The Anywaa people live along the rivers, which is one of the reasons that made Nuer people interested in occupying Anywaa lands. The lands are green with grass, right by the rivers which make them suitable for cattle, especially during the dry season of the year.

For instance, the Dikony River (Akobo River) made Akobo very attractive to the Nuer because of the green grass and water it provides during the dry season of the year. The Nuer emigrated to this land in big numbers making the local Anywaa vulnerable as they were outnumbered. When interviewed by Perner in 1976, Chief Ading expressed his fear that the Nuer arriving in Akobo in increasingly higher numbers would make them the majority in Akobo town "soon."[6] Unsurprisingly, the population of Nuer exponentially increased throughout the years in Akobo town, surpassing the local Anywaa population. Thus, they killed the Anywaa people, assimilated those who stayed, and forced the Anywaa out of Akobo. Today,

---

5. Opap, *Unsung Giants*, 45–46.
6. Perner, *Why Did You Come If You Leave Again*, 98.

Akobo land is mostly occupied by the Nuer people and a few assimilated Anywaa people who refused to leave. The tactic that the Nuer used to invade Anywaa lands, specifically Akobo and Chiro, was not through their military might but a friendly approach. As King Agada stated, the Anywaa fought and defended their lands when the Nuer tried to invade the lands through military means. Six great wars were fought against the Nuer, and five of them were won by the Anywaa people. Acquiring weapons from the Abyssinian empire, King Odiel Kwot from Abwobo became the first Anywaa king to open an organized attack against the Jikany Nuers using rifles.[7] Following King Odiel Kwot, King Oliimi from Akobo (a cousin of Odiel from his father's side) also attacked the Jikany Nuer. Despite a strong military resistance of the Anywaa kings, the Nuer people were successful in conquering Anywaa lands through deceptive peaceful tactics.

During the dry seasons, the Nuer would emigrate to Anywaa lands with their cattle and make a peaceful agreement with the Anywaa chiefs. They would send people to the Anywaa chiefs and ask them if they could come to the land for grazing during the three months of the dry season, mostly from June to September. To be accepted by the chiefs, they would send people with gifts, which were mostly cows. After showering the chiefs with the gifts, the chiefs would allow them to stay in the land until they returned to their country after the dry season was over. This created friendships between the Nuer and local chiefs, and they were allowed to settle closer to the river on the Anywaa land with the chiefs' approvals. The Anywaa people also allowed them to use their farms as camps for their cattle so that the manures that cattle leave behind would then yield in high crops during harvesting time.

During my interview with Oron Ochala, he stated:

> The first time I saw Nuer in Gambella was in the 1970 Ethiopian Calendar (1977). When they came, they were walking naked with their cattle. They went to the chief of Cham village and asked him for his permission to stay along the Openo bank so their cattle would graze there throughout the summer. When the summer was over, they went back to Bentiu, Southern Sudan, and came back the next year. They built up friendships with the chiefs or leaders of kebele in this way.[8]

---

7. Opap, *Unsung Giants*, 46
8. Interview with Oron Ochala (Apr 26, 2022).

To create stronger bonds, they would sometimes leave their wives or daughters with the chiefs or chosen "Anywaa friends." When they came back the following year and found their wife pregnant or with a new baby, they would take back their wives including the kids. They also would purposefully give their wives to any male they found tall and attractive for the night, hoping that he would impregnate the wife. When they get pregnant, they would take the child and assimilate him/her. In the Anywaa tradition, you have to be born from an Anywaa mother and father in order to be considered Anywaa. If you are mixed, you would not be considered pure Anywaa, and you would be often referred to as *Jur*, which means "foreigner." Thus, children who were half-Anywaa and half-Nuer would be considered Nuer by the Anywaa people and treated like one. This approach had made the Nuer build friendships with many leaders in the Anywaa lands of Baat-Openo, and they were allowed to settle with their cattle in Nyium and Akobo. Later on, a smaller number of them were also allowed by the Anywaa people to settle in Jikaw. In return, they showered the leaders with gifts of cattle. But little by little, their numbers increased, and they acquired more lands. They also started making alliances with the Anywaa villages. Perner stated:

> It happened that the Nuer would make friends with an Anyuak family and thus be allowed to move next to them. By and by, other relatives would join them, until the Nuer would become the majority. This may have happened in Nasir, and later on it would happen in Akobo, which eventually was "swallowed" by the Nuer as well and would even become one of the Nuer strongholds in the region.[9]

Historically, the Anywaa chiefs and kings ruled their different villages independently. So, every village had nobility in competition with one another, seeking superiority over others. This gave the Nuer a great opportunity to divide the Anywaa people even more and strengthen their relationship with the villages that they settled by. For example, in his paper, Agalu stated:

> The Anuak villages such as Pinymoo and Imedho had alliances with villages of Nuer, Canngac and Puldeng respectively. When the two villages fought, Canngac were supplying guns to Pinymoo and Puldeng did the same to Imedho.[10]

---

9. Perner, *Why Did You Come If You Leave Again*, 90.
10. Agula, "Interaction and Conflict among the Nuer and Anuak," 3.

As the Anywaa people kept fighting among themselves, their population kept dwindling while the Nuer population increased. Soon, the Nuer would take over the Anywaa villages and assimilate those who refused to leave. Many Anywaa lands were destroyed by the Nuer in this way. The Nuer aggression and expansionism was historical, and the Anywaa kings and chiefs resisted it for centuries. According to Gebeyehu the first attack was launched by the Nuer in the 1870s, and they continued through the 1880s when the Nuer of Jikany migrated east from Southern Sudan.[11]

The Anywaa had an upper hand and took back some of the lands when they received weapons from the highlanders (the Abyssinian Empire). The king of Abwobo, Odiel Kwot, received weapons from the highlanders, specifically the Oromo. King Odiel used these rifles to fight back the Nuer of Gajaak in the nineteenth century. King Oliimi war-Agaanya also acquired weapons from the highlanders. But Oliimi fought the other Anywaa kings with the new rifles he received from the highlanders to gain superiority over his rivals. Gebeyehu stated:

> Oliimi didn't use his rifles to invade the Nuer. Rather, he raided other Anuak villages. He forced one noble living south of Akobo, Akway (Akwai) wa-Cam, to flee to the highland of Ethiopia.[12]

King Oliimi did fight the Jikany Nuer, while also attacking other Anywaa kings competing for the ocwok (*uchuok*). He ruled Ajwaara in the Adongo region. But with the rifles he received from the highlanders, he moved on to control Digira in the Tiernam region.[13] This internal conflict between the Anywaa kings and chiefs helped the Nuer advance deeper into Anywaa lands. However, in 1912, King Oliimi carried out an attack against the Gaajak Nuer and was killed during the fight. According to Gebeyehu, the Anywaa conducted raids against the Nuer in 1906, 1910, 1911, and 1931. The Anywaa were successful in preventing the Nuer expansion and reclaiming lands that were already taken by the Nuer. As they gained more weapons, they destroyed the Nuer and pushed them back. When King Akway-wa-Cham took over Adongo Kingdom after the death of King Oliimi, he armed three hundred followers with rifles and attacked several Nuer settlements. In 1911, King Akway attacked the Lou Nuer and defeated them. The Nuer suffered a heavy loss and a large number of their cattle, children, and

---

11. Gebeyehu, "Ethnic Conflict," 101.
12. Gebeyehu, "Ethnic Conflict," 101.
13. Opap, *Unsung Giants*, 51

women were captured by King Akway. This had caused tremendous anger in Sudan's government, which pushed the British to act against the Anywaa Kingdom in Adongo. I will discuss more about this in the next chapter.

The abolition of the Anywaa monarchy by the Derg regime had created a great opportunity for the Nuer to increase their advancement deeper into Anywaa lands. This was the beginning of weakening of the Anywaa people and the fall of the Anywaa kingdoms. When the first civil war broke out in Sudan in 1955, the Nuer refugees started encroaching into the Anywaa lands in large numbers. The population of Nuer settlers in Anywaa lands dramatically expanded in the 1960s, and they renamed some of the Anywaa villages into the Nuer language.[14] The war in Sudan gave the Nuer a great opportunity to move deeper into Anywaa lands with the permission of the Ethiopian government under international refugee laws. The Nuer refugees had no intention of going back to Sudan, as this program gave them a great opportunity to settle in the Anywaa lands which they had been forcefully trying to occupy for centuries. On the other hand, the Derg regime had a goal of *Ethiopianizing* Gambella, which was to change the face of Gambella to look more like "Ethiopia" by increasing the population of highlanders in the region.

In their plans, the Nuer have laid out eight points that Nuer people must follow to take over the Anywaa lands:

1. Every Nuer must know that the Anuaks are his traditional enemy and that our colonization, invasion, and assimilation plan must be applied to all Anuak regions both in Ethiopia and Sudan.

2. Every Nuer must know thoroughly, and reply to the Anuaks and other ethnic groups surrounding them, the methods used successfully to conquer Nyium Amiel (currently Nasir), Akobo (Sudan side), and Adura, Akobo (Ethiopia side). You must proceed with methods and gradually refrain from any precipitation, which might awaken the spectra of the Great Conqueror Latgur, our national hero.

3. Every Nuer intellectual must adopt as his first goal the control of additional districts, as everybody is aware of the importance of controlling local seats of authority to spread political ideas into the uneducated populace.

---

14. Feyissa, *Playing Different Games*, 120.

4. Every Nuer intellectual must make friends within the Anuak administration and get acquainted with the bureaucratic process and thus prepare himself for eventual takeover in which he is expected to take the place and eventually head the whole department.

5. Since we cannot replace the Anuak representatives just elected and put our own people in their places, let's make them our friends. We must conquer them by offering them gifts like cows and alcohol. Arrange marriages with their women as we have been doing successfully on the Sudan side. They will not resist our wealth; this must be applied mostly in their big towns like Gambella, both Akobo and Pochalla.

6. When the control of all-important positions is achieved, we must remove all our traditional enemies easily.

7. With regard to conquering the Anuaks, you must use the "blood exchange pact" in which Anuaks foolishly believe.

8. Avail yourselves of the credulity of the Anuak elites and use them to promote our interest and to look credible in electoral drives. As soon as the electoral drives are over, they bilk them to show their inefficiency (this article must mostly apply on the Gambella, Ethiopia, side).[15]

These points to eliminate the Anywaa people from their lands made the Anywaa people viewed the Nuer as one of their most dangerous enemies. For the Anywaa people, land is their life and identity. The Nuer, on the other hand, believe in taking lands from others. They are following their plan of pushing the Anywaa people all the way to Tier-Agak. They successfully followed these eight points and accomplished almost all of them including pushing the Anywaa people all the way to Tier-Agak in Gambella town. According to Dereje Feyissa there were no Nuer residents in Gambella in 1942 except those who came for cattle trade.[16] After they sell their cattle, they go back to the Nuer land, Bentiu. The inhibition of Cangkwaar by the refugee Nuer students, as well as renaming it to Newland, was a great success that Thuwat Pal and Opal Lual[17] worked on, paving the way for a

---

15. These eight points were discovered in a letter that the Anywaa people believed was written by the Nuer elites. It was first discovered by the Anywaa people in the United States in 2000. And it was discussed by the Anywaa Community Association in North America (ACANA) during one of their meetings in Minnesota.

16. Feyissa, *Playing Different Games*, 129.

17. Opal was the son of Lual, who was an Anywaa person. Opal was an Anywaa son from Anywaa family in Akobo. When he was captured by the Nuer during a fight, he was

The Anywaa Relationship with Murle and Nuer People

massive number of Nuer to settle in Gambella town. Their next step would be to increase their kebeles in Gambella town while trying to reach the Anywaa land in Lul (Anywaa zone and woredas), and Pochalla, which is the heart of Anywaa land that still maintains its monarchy system.

---

then assimilated by the Nuer and had *gar* (marks on the forehead). Opal became Nuer and was also considered by the Anywaa people as Nuer since he was marked and had *gar*. He changed his name to Joshua Delual. Opal ruled Gambella as a governor during the Derg government in the 1980s and worked along with Thuwat Pal (a Nuer politician).

Mr. Oron Ochala was a very active leader in the Anywaa community and Mekane Yesus Church in Gambella. After the Anywaa genocide, he moved to a Kenya refugee camp and was granted asylum in the United States with his family. He served the Anywaa Community in North America (ACANA) as president of the organization for many years. I interviewed him on April 26, 2022.

Chapter 2

The Anywaa Country and British Colonial

The Anywaa Kingdoms

THE ANYWAA PEOPLE LIVE along the rivers at the border of Ethiopia and Sudan: Openo (Baro in Amharic), Gilo, Alworo, Akobo, Oboth, Dikony, and Agweny. They have twelve clans, which they called *Dhøk-uudï*. Those clans are Jo-waat Cwaay, Jo-waat Naadhi, Jo-waat Maaro, Jo-waat Jango, Jo-po Nguu, Jo-waat Maalo, Jo-waat Tong, Jo-waat luala, Jo-waat Kaanyo, Jo-waat Twua, Jo-waat Naamo, and Jo-waat Mwungo. The Anywaa people have two political structures which they used to rule themselves with for centuries: *nyec* and *kwar*, which are kingship and headmanship respectively. *Nyeye* and *kwaari* ruled Anywaa lands in a very organized and well-structured government system for centuries.

The structure of *nyec* includes *nyeya* (king), and he is the head of the nation. *Nyec* is passed on through the family line; *nyibur* (Prime Minister); *nyikugo* (king's deputy); *nyitheengngo* (deputy of *nyikugo*); *nyiiatwiel* (Minister of Interior and Public Relations); *nyiiatwiel mar bat-boogi* (deputy); *nyikeeno* (food service affairs); *deputy of nyikeeno* (cook/chef); *kwaac kodo* (drum beater/whistle-blower); *mee* (king's maternal uncles); *katha-radhi/kwaac-lwaak* (general chief of staff); deputy *katha radhi*; *lwaak mar kaadi* (military intelligence); *lwaak-gan-dwong* (special forces); *lwaak-nga-apeiya* (all royal guards); *nyipeem* (prince), and *bimm* (tax collector).[1] Kwar has a similar structure to the structure of Nyec. The system of Kwar contains *kwaaro/rwoth* as the head or the leader of one village. Just like the nyec system, kwar also has *nyikugo, nyibur, nyiiatwiel, kwaac-lwaak, kar wang* (security advisor to the headman), *nyibaatbogo* (social secretary and servant to the headman), *nyikeeno*, and *nyikeeno mano teedo* (cook/chef). Despite the similarity between the two political structures, there are a few major differences between nyeye and kwaari. Nyeye ruled multiple territories while kwaari only ruled over the villages that they were staying in. In addition to that, you must be born from a certain clan (*dhi-ØtØ*) to be appointed as king. This *dhi-ØtØ* is known as *dhi-Øt nyec*. But kwaari could come from multiple clans.

Nyeye and *kwaari* ruled their specific villages without occupying or expanding their territory due to their respect for borders, which the Anywaa people called *keew*. Expanding into the territory of another king or chief was considered a threat or aggression which would lead to two things: it could be resolved either through diplomacy and talk or by military action because it is considered as a violation of territorial sovereignty. In the Anywaa tradition, kings ruled large areas and many villages compared to the Anywaa chiefs. Even though each leader is within his own area, they sometimes had to compete for the royal emblems. The respect for borders and territories was also very important to the Anywaa people, and any violation of territorial integrity by another king or chief would lead to a bigger conflict. If one person commits a crime in an area under one chief or king and they escape into the land under a different king or chief, they will automatically get protection from the king/chief of that area. When one king/chief wants to pass through a land that is not under their control, they must ask for permission from the king/chief who controls that specific area.

The competition for royal emblems, power, and superiority caused big conflicts between the Anywaa kings and chiefs who were ruling different territories. There are two very important beads that show royal emblems, and each king or chief must wear them to show their nobility. The beads are *ocwok* for *nyeye* and *abudho* for *kwaari*. The king and chief who have the *ocwok* and *abudho* respectively in their possession would have the glory and power that comes with it. The royal emblems are not monopolized entirely by the *nyenya* (the king who control *ocwok*) because he is required to allow

---

1. Opap, *Unsung Giants*, 101–3

other *nyeye* to wear *ocwok* to demonstrate their nobility as well.[2] However, some *nyeye* would hold onto the bead for a long time to demonstrate their power. This had caused wars between the Anywaa kings because *ocwok* is only possessed by the strongest king, which would make them powerful over other kings. *Nyeye* ruled the entire east and southeast of the Anywaa lands, and *kwaari* ruled the rest of the Anywaa lands.

The Expansion of the Ethiopian State to the Anywaa Land and the Defeat of the British Armies

The natural resources and the geographical location of Anywaa land attracted much attention from both the Sudan government which was under the imperial rule of the British and the Abyssinian Empire. The geographical location of the Anywaa people put them in a dangerous situation, in which they had to be aggressive to survive as people. As Jessen stated during his observation in 1904:

> There is no doubt that these people, who, sad to say, are gradually becoming extinct, are greatly influenced by their surroundings and the peculiar circumstances in which they are placed. Shut on one side by the giant Abyssinian mountains, and on the other by the warlike and ever-aggressive Nuer tribes, their existence is not much better than that of the flying fish.[3]

Before acquiring weapons from the Oromo in late 1800, the Anywaa people experienced great encroachments by the Nuer from the Sudan side, and they also faced kidnapping and raidings from the highlanders from the Abyssinian Empire. According to an interview of Kurimoto with Prince Ojwanga Gilo, the grandson of King Odiel, the Anywaa people fought the Oromo of Gore when they first encountered them on Anywaa land. At this time, the Anywaa people of Abwobo were only using traditional spears, and Ngeynyo, the father of Odiel, was the king. According to Ojwanga, the raiders wanted to take people into slavery, but they were defeated and were chased up to Bure. Ojwanga said, "They came to capture people, take them to their home and make them slaves."[4] Villages like Diipa by lake Thatha,

---

2. Feyissa, *Playing Different Games*, 42.
3. Jessen, "South-western Abyssinia," 162–63.
4. Kurimoto, "Natives and Outsiders," 19.

and Gog were raided by Ras Tesemma of Gore and Abyssinians respectively.[5] Many people were killed, and the number of people who were captured as slaves was not documented. Even after the Anywaa people obtained firearms, there were raids attempted but were not successful due to resistance. For instance, the men of Tokkon, the Oromo Balabat of Bure, raided the village of Itang in 1905, only killing twenty-four Anywaa people.[6] The number of casualties on the Anywaa side was smaller due to the resistance, but the casualties among Tokkon's men were not recorded.

When King Odiel took the throne after his father died, he created a good relationship between the Anywaa and Oromo. This relationship was created based on mutual and reciprocal benefits. The Anywaa land, Gambella, was used by the Oromo people for hunting buffalo, and the Anywaa people got rifles from the Oromo. The Anywaa Kingdom traded buffalo heads, honey, leopard skins, and ivory with the Oromos. In return, the Anywaa received rifles, salt, beads, clothes, sugar, and tobacco (*athamgaala*). This mutual relationship went on for nearly a century between 1880 and 1960 between the Anywaa kingdom and the Ethiopians in Bure, Gora, and Sayo (Dembi Dollo).[7] The king of Abwobo, King Odiel, became the first king in the Anywaa kingdom to create a relationship with the Ethiopians. He then became the most powerful king in the Anywaa nation in 1897 and controlled the royal emblems for a very long time.[8] King Odiel became too powerful after creating a relationship with the Oromo people and the imperial Ethiopia and became the first Anywaa king to acquire rifles from the imperial Ethiopia. Following king Odiel Kwot of Abwobo, king Oliimi Wara Aganya of Akobo and king Akway Cham of Adongo reached Imperial Ethiopia and created a relationship to acquire rifles. Those two kings became powerful as well. Those three powerful kings emerged in the first decade of the twentieth century and took offensive attacks against the Nuer tribe.[9] This had decelerated the Nuer expansion into the Anywaa lands as they fled the Arabs and also searched for green lands for their cattle in the east, leaving their home: Bentiu. The Nuer people who were using spears suffered great losses as the Anywaa kings acquired more weapons from the Abyssinian Empire.

5. Kurimoto, "Natives and Outsiders," 12.
6. Kurimoto, "Natives and Outsiders," 12.
7. Opap, *Unsung Giants*, 37.
8. Opap, *Unsung Giants*, 39.
9. Feyissa, *Playing Different Games*, 123.

The trade relationship with imperial Ethiopia has helped the Anywaa kings build and strengthen their military capability. In about 1911, the total number of rifles in Anywaa possession was estimated at between 10,000 and 25,000.[10] This had become a huge threat to the British, which led to diplomatic talks between the British Kingdom and imperial Ethiopia with the goal to disarm the Anywaa people. In his book, Dereje Feyissa stated that "Disarm the Anywaa" was the British political pre-occupation in the 1910s and 1920s. This was due to the resistance they faced from the king Akway Cham of Otaalo, Adongo. The British colonial forces attacked the kingdom of Adongo in 1912 after King Adongo Cham attacked the Lou Nuer invaders in 1911 and captured up to two thousand cattle. He also captured a large number of women, men and children. After capturing hundreds of Nuer men, women, and children, King Akway sold them as slaves to the *gaala*. Since the Nuer were under the British colony, the British were forced to fight back in order to retrieve the cattle and Nuer who were captured by King Akway. The British army that marched to Otaalo on March 15 included 11 British, 21 Egyptian officers, and 407 members of other ranks.[11] The army of King Akway Cham went out to meet the British and caused heavy damage to the British colonial military at the battle of Juom, close to Otaalo village. In his interview with Okoth Owity, King Akway Agada stated that over one hundred forces from the British side were killed because more than one hundred rifles were captured.[12] The British lost four commissioned and thirty-seven non-commissioned officers during the battle. This defeat caused a great embarrassment and humiliation to the British Kingdom, which led them to pursue a diplomatic way to resolve the Anywaa threat.

The British underestimated the Anywaa military power, which cost them many lives, including the British officers. The British launched a diplomatic offensive to corner Anywaa people, but imperial Ethiopia was initially not interested in pursuing any military conflict with the Anywaa kingdom. This was due to the ivory trade between the Anywaa kingdom and imperial Ethiopia. Even though he tried to detain the Anywaa kings (Odiel and Akway), King Menelik II still wanted to keep the mutual trade (ivory-guns) between the two kingdoms since Anywaa lands were the main source for ivory. When the diplomatic way failed with the Abyssinian

---

10. Feyissa, *Playing Different Games*, 123.
11. Feyissa, *Playing Different Games*, 123–24.
12. Opap, *Unsung Giants*, 53.

Empire, the British prepared to invade and destroy the Anywaa kingdom. But before attacking King Akway, World War I took place in 1914 which diverted the attention of the British. The relationship between imperial Ethiopia and the Anywaa kingdoms hit a dead end when imperial Ethiopia started forcing the Anywaa people to submit to it later, after the Anglo-Ethiopian agreement in 1902, and pay taxes to the central government. The Anglo-Ethiopian agreement was negotiated by King Menelik II and the British without the knowledge of the Anywaa people. In the agreement, Gambella was given to imperial Ethiopia by the British in exchange for Kassala, which is in the northern border of the two empires.[13] Despite the agreement made by these two empires, the Anywaa people continued to independently control their lands without any foreign military presence in their occupied territories until 1920s. When king Akway died in 1920, he was replaced by his son Cham. Cham was a very young boy at the age of twelve when he became a king. So, the British used this opportunity to weaken the Anywaa kingdom in Adongo by taking the *ocwok*.

The first encounter with Ethiopia took place when the delegations of the ruler of Itang, Ray Gilo, were captured by the Ethiopian forces on their way to Gambella town. In Okoth Owity's interview with Obang Okumu Okom on April 27, 2019, Obang stated:

> Ray Gilo sent his people to Gambella but before reaching Gambella town, his delegations were arrested by the Ethiopian military.[14]

Chief Ray Gilo peacefully asked imperial Ethiopia to release his people, but his request was denied. Ray Gilo ended up sending his forces to Koi and attacked Ethiopian forces, destroyed the camp, and returned his captured people to Itang. This attack sent a message to imperial Ethiopia that the Anywaa people would not tolerate unlawful detention of their people and any intrusion into their lands. It also challenged the power of imperial Ethiopia to implement the agreement they signed with the British which gave them control over the Anywaa land, Gambella. The growth of Anywaa military power threatened imperial Ethiopia, which forced them to try to prevent the Anywaa people from becoming too powerful. King Menelik II started trying to weaken the Anywaa military by imprisoning King Odiel and king Akway. Even though King Odiel had a good relationship with Ras Tesemma of Gore in the beginning, he was imprisoned by the Abyssinian

---

13. Cascão, "Resource-based Conflict," 153.
14. Opap, *Unsung Giants*, 128.

Empire in 1905 or 1906 for about four years.[15] King Odiel's imprisonment and the disarmament of his people was purposefully done by the Abyssinian empire to weaken him. When he was released, King Odiel died or went back to the river in 1919. The decline of King Odiel's power after he was imprisoned led to the rise of King Akway and King Oliimi.

When King Akway became too powerful, he was imprisoned at Bure by Ras Tassamma. However, he was able to escape in 1909.[16-17] According to Dereje Feyissa, King Akway took revenge by fighting the imperial forces in Gambella and killed Lij Kassa, the imperial agent who was the government representative in Gambella in 1913.[18] However, according to historians like Kurimoto, Lij Kassa was killed in another battle in Pinykeew.[19] Lij Kassa was trying to collect *gimmira* from Kwaaro Ojulu wor-Obulu when the fighting took place. The battle took place when Gaala (Kassa's soldier) beat a sick Anywaa woman with a whip by the river. An Anywaa man stepped in and beat Gaala with a stick until he bled in his head. At that time, Gaala shot the man, and the Kwaaro sent his men to fight Gaale. According to an interview done by Kurimoto with Obala Ojulu (October 12, 1990), Obala stated that the battle was fought by the back of the river. When Gaale tried to surrender by going out to the Anywaa carrying grass in their hands (a sign of surrender), they were all gunned down, and only one man survived. This battle is what most Anywaa recall and passed on orally. The Anywaa of Pinykeew killed Lij Kassa and his men because they didn't want to pay any tribute to Ethiopia as they viewed it as *adima* (oppression).

Thus, four thousand spearmen and one thousand riflemen were sent to Gambella under the command of *fitawrari* Solomon, the son of Jote Tulu who was the governor of Sayyo in western Wollega. When he tried to fight King Akway, Fitawrari Solomon was defeated by King Akway's forces and lost more than one hundred of his fighters. *Fitawrari* Solomon was so confounded by the fighting skill of the Anywaa, and the excuse that he found for his defeat was to accuse the Greek manager of the Openo Syndicate of supplying Anywaa with twenty thousand rounds of ammunition and

---

15. Kurimoto, "Natives and Outsiders," 13–14.

16. Kurimoto, "Natives and Outsiders," 14.

17. In another source, Bahru Zewde (1976) wrote in his book that King Akway escaped prison in Bure in 1903.

18. Feyissa, *Playing Different Games*, 124.

19. Kurimoto, "Natives and Outsiders," 25–26.

teaching them the technique of firing from rifle-pits.[20] As a result, Solomon burned down huts in Gambella that belonged to the syndicate. So, the forces of king Akway proceeded and took over the trade route along the Openo river in Gambella and Akobo rivers.[21] This had angered the imperial Ethiopia and they prepared more and organized another attack to force the Anywaa people into submission and give their taxes to the Abyssinian Empire.

In 1914, Majid Abud, who was a Druze Syrian working for imperial Ethiopia, was sent to Gambella to carry out the new mission of forcing the Anywaa people into submission. Majid had a good relationship with King Odiel and the Anywaa of Bonga. As a result, the forces of King Odiel and the Anywaa of Bonga collaborated with Majid's forces and raided other parts of Anywaa land. Even though he had a very little army with him when he arrived in Gambella, he forcefully conscripted the Anywaa of Bonga to increase his forces. In addition to that, volunteer soldiers from King Odiel joined Majid's force and the number of his total forces reached to some 1400 riflemen.[22] The leader of Itang, Ray Gilo, rejected Majid Abud's mission, and prepared for the war. On March 20 and 21, 1916, the battle of Itang took place between Majid's forces and the people of Itang. As a result of long preparation by *qenyazmach* (commander of the right), Majid Abud and a large number of well-equipped militaries, the people of Itang were overwhelmed and defeated by imperial Ethiopia after a long and bloody war. The Burayu men were the first to attack the people of Itang, and they were nearly wiped out by the Anywaa fighters. When the forces of Majid and the Anfillo contingent arrived, they joined the Burayu men and overwhelmed the Anywaa forces. The forces of King Odiel were also collaborating with Majid's forces due to the friendship that they had at that time. The Anywaa of Itang lost 532 men, and 500 men were castrated. But Majid only lost fifty men from his side.[23] This catastrophic loss sent a clear message to the Anywaa people who resisted, and the message was to voluntarily submit to Ethiopia or the Anywaa land, Gambella, would be forcefully incorporated into the Ethiopian state. Majid's main targets were the most powerful *kwaaro* (chief) of Baat-Openo, Ojulu wor-Obulu, and the most powerful Anywaa king who maintained Anywaa independence, King

20. Zewde, "Relations Between Ethiopia and the Sudan," 135.
21. Feyissa, *Playing Different Games*, 124.
22. Zewde, "Relations Between Ethiopia and the Sudan," 141.
23. Kurimoto, "Natives and Outsiders," 29.

Akway. That defeat didn't stop the Anywaa people from defending their lands against imperial Ethiopia.

After the defeat of the Anywaa of Itang by Majid Abud, imperial Ethiopia created police stations throughout Anywaa lands in Baat-Openo. After the people of Itang and Puol suffered a great loss, Majid went on along with forces that also included King Odiel's forces to fight King Akway in Adongo district. But Majid faced a disastrous defeat by king Akway and he narrowly escaped death. On September 2, 1991, Ojulu Deng narrated the battle as follows:

> A man called Majid came from Ethiopia. When Majid came, he proceeded to Adongo to a nyeya Akwai Wo-Cham. When they fought, he didn't defeat Akwai and came back. He went back again. When he went back again and fought, he didn't defeat Adongo. Majid came back through Jor and came along the river [Openo]. When Majid reached Puol, he caught the Kwaaro of Puol. He fought Jo-Puol and Jo-Itang and Majid's men were finished there as they fought very much. Majid was missed with one of his friends. When he came and reached Obit [a place in Pinykeew] here, he sent a man. He reached Mori and said, 'People were finished. Majid is there.' Majid was a white man. He was not an Amhara. Only his men were jo-Ethiopia, Amhara . . .[24]

The defeat of Majid and his forces by King Akway and the people of Puol and Itang was a great failure for Majid to achieve his goal of bringing the Anywaa powerful king and chief to submission. Majid was then replaced by imperial Ethiopia, and he left Gambella in June of 1916. The person who replaced him was Fitawrari Fanta. When Majid went back to Gambella in 1932, he continued collaborating with the king of Abwobo, Gilo. King Gilo was the king who replaced King Ogwak. King Ogwak replaced King Odiel, but Gilo rebelled against him. Gilo went on and attacked King Ogwak on his way when he was returning from Adongo. When he couldn't defeat King Ogwak, Gilo went to Gore and accused King Ogwak of arresting Oromo messengers and enslaving Majang captives.[25] So, King Ogwok was arrested and put in jail in Gore, and Gilo became the king of Abwobo. King Gilo controlled Abwobo until he died in late 1960s.

Majid was sent back to Gambella in 1932 after the Anywaa people on Ethiopia side carried out extensive raids on the Murle (Beir) inside Sudan's

---

24. Kurimoto, "Natives and Outsiders," 28.
25. Kurimoto, "Natives and Outsiders," 30.

territory in March 1932.²⁶ This raid devastated the Murle, and many of them were killed. Their women, children, and about eight hundred head of cattle were captured by Anywaa forces. According to Bahru, this attack resulted in a huge protest by the Sudan government against the central government of Ethiopia in Addis Ababa. Thus, the government of Ethiopia was forced to pay compensation to the government of Sudan after the meeting that was held in Gambella in June 1932 between the delegation led by A. G. Pawson (governor of Upper Nile), Ras Mulugeta (governor of Illubabor), and Fitawrari Hayla Maryam (the governor of Sayo).²⁷ In addition to paying compensation for the dead Murle, Ethiopia was forced to repatriate cattle and Murle who were held captives by the Anywaa. After taking responsibility and agreeing to compensate the government of Sudan, the government of Ethiopia needed to have someone who could represent these demands to the Anywaa people and return the Murle captives and their cattle back to the Sudanese government. Majid was then sent to Gambella to carry out the implementation of the agreement. When he arrived in Gambella, Majid took two Anywaa kwaari who were leading the raid of Murle with him to Gore. His main goal was to attack the people of Ajwaara, Nyikaani, and Tor.

Majid had a force consisting of Baqo Zabana (guards of lowlands), and some three hundred to four hundred troops who were trained in Addis Ababa.²⁸ To compensate for the Murle who were killed during the Anywaa raids, Majid attacked the people of Tor and captured their cattle. In 1934, a large Abyssinian force was sent against the headman of Itang in Baat-Openo, but they were not successful. When they reached Itang, they were met by the Anywaa forces and defeated by the headman of Itang. Sixty Abyssinian troops were killed during the battle.²⁹ The Anywaa forces continued to use guerrilla warfare and constantly raided the police stations in Gog, Itang, and Pokumo during 1952–58. Even though imperial Ethiopia successfully forced the Anywaa people to succumb to Ethiopia's statehood, the resistance continued in many places. For instance, the Anywaa people in Pokumo continued to fight the Ethiopian forces who were trying to open a police station in the area. This resistance was led by kwaaro Atong Abula. The struggle ended in the 1960s when Pokumo was burned down by the

26. Zewde, "Relations Between Ethiopia and Sudan," 156.
27. Zewde, "Relations Between Ethiopia and Sudan," 157–58.
28. Zewde, "Relations Between Ethiopia and Sudan," 160.
29. Evans-Pritchard, *Political System of the Anuak*, 13.

army from Gore, and it was renamed *Birhaneselam*.[30] The destruction of Pokumo was a great political defeat which was followed by oppression from imperial Ethiopia as there was no organized force to challenge the Abyssinian Empire in the area anymore. Those who were not able to pay taxes had to go to Oromia land such as Welega and work in coffee plantations. When they got money, they would pay taxes to imperial Ethiopia. Unlike the Anywaa kingdoms and their military might, there were other smaller ethnic groups in Gambella who endured intensive kidnapping and slavery under the Abyssinian empire without defending themselves. The Majang, Opwo, and Komo didn't have any organized governmental structure to govern themselves, and they also lived in isolated areas deep in the forests in smaller groups. Thus, they became more vulnerable to imperial Ethiopia and the slave raiders.

---

30. Feyissa, *Playing Different Games*, 126. *Birhaneselam* is an Amharic word meaning "the light of peace."

Chapter 3

Slavery under Imperial Ethiopia

SLAVERY AND THE EXPORT of slaves goes back to the Aksumite Kingdom (100–940 AD). But in this chapter, I focus more on slavery in imperial Ethiopia throughout the nineteenth and early twentieth centuries. During this period, owning slaves was viewed as a symbol of having high status. Wealthy people such as emperors, landlords, judges, and rich peasants had slaves who worked for them. Those who were captured as prisoners of war (POWs) were also forced into slavery. Some people were forced into temporary slavery to pay off debts (debt bondage) that they owe, or to pay their taxes. The slave trade was also a big part of the economy during imperial Ethiopia due to the taxes the central government collected from the trade. Thus, slave trade was common under rulers such as Sahle Sellassie, Theodrore, Yohannes, and Menelik who followed the tradition of their country.[1] Even though they attempted to prohibit slavery, they were unsuccessful until Emperor Haile Selassie abolished it in 1942. Christianity played a great role in justifying the slavery during imperial Ethiopia. For instance, according to Pankhurst, *Fetha Nagast* (the law of the kings) recognized and accepted slavery.[2] It also gave the institution authority to use quotes from Scripture, stating:

> Both thy bond-men and thy bond-maids, which thou shall have, shall be of the heathen that are round about you; of them shall ye buy, and of their families that are with you, which they begat in

---

1. Pankhurst, "Ethiopian Slave Trade," 220.
2. Pankhurst, "Ethiopian Slave Trade," 220.

your land; and they shall be your possession. And ye shall take them as an inheritance for your children after you; they shall be your bond-men forever. Leviticus 25:44–46.

The rulers and wealthy people used these words to justify their roles in keeping slaves for themselves. Though the slaves came from many different territories under and around the Abyssinian Empire, there were common places that were used as reservoirs for slaves. For instance, the people who were enslaved in the capital of Shewa, Ankobar, during the early nineteenth century were mostly the Gallas, Shanqellas, Gurages, and people from Janjero and Enarea.[3] The word *Galla* was used during the Abyssinian empire to refer to the Oromos. The Oromos are the largest ethnic group in Ethiopia, and their small population reside in Kenya. The word *Shanqella* was used to refer to dark-skinned people or the Nilotic groups from the western part of Ethiopia. Today, these two words (Galla and Shanqella) are commonly used in a derogatory way to insult someone as "bariya" or a slave. According to Dr. Merab, the people who were forced into slavery and did the labor works in Addis Ababa were mainly the Gallas, Gurages, Shanqellas, Benishanguls, and Walamos.[4] The provinces in the south and west were used as the main places to raid and capture slaves. The Kunama (dark-skinned people) of northwest Ethiopia and Eritrea were also heavily raided and enslaved; thus their very name came to mean "slave."[5] Gambella is one of the provinces in the southwestern part of Ethiopia. The four main indigenous ethnic groups that inhabit Gambella during the era of imperial Ethiopia were Anywaa, Komo, Opwo, and Majang. The Nuer are latecomers who settled in Gambella after the civil war that took place in Sudan in the 1950s. There are also other small populations such as Olaam, Dhwok, Maw, and Bula that live in Gambella. The people of Gambella belong to the Nilotic group, and they are dark-skinned people.

During the Abyssinian empire, the skin color of those Nilotic would make them be considered "shanqella" or slaves by default. Throughout the nineteenth and early twentieth centuries, the Anywaa kingdom was one of the strongest kingdoms in the southwest of imperial Ethiopia. Therefore, they were less likely to be raided by the slave raiders compared to the other Nilotic groups with no form of structural government. Living together in villages made the Anywaa people also less likely to be raided. According to

3. Pankhurst, "Ethiopian Slave Trade," 221.
4. Pankhurst, "Ethiopian Slave Trade," 221.
5. Campbell et al., *Women and Slavery*, 216.

Bahru Zewde, the Anywaa prevented massive enslavement due to their dint of courageous struggle as well as the geographical protection.[6] However, they were vulnerable when they were traveling from one village to another in small numbers. Before the deterioration of the Anywaa country's relationship with the Abyssinian Empire, the Anywaa kings were also involved in selling the Nuer and Murle war prisoners to the Abyssinian empire as slaves. Though the Anywaa people denied their involvement with the Abyssinian Empire slave trade, they exchanged war prisoners with guns. As Perner stated:

> Some of the information would not only help me to understand better but would even allow me to rectify some incorrect statements. For example, the Anywuak firmly denied having been actively involved in the slave trade while in fact they had sold their prisoners as slaves to Ethiopia in exchange for guns.[7]

The Anywaa people who were living outside the villages and those who were traveling became vulnerable and the main target of the Amhara slavers. To protect themselves and their children, the Anywaa people traveled or went hunting in groups. They also built their huts closer in their villages, giving them protection against the Abyssinian slave raiders. There were also people in between some villages that the Anywaa people referred to as *jo-kwori*. Those were people from the community who had debts or committed serious crimes and decided to leave society. They usually stay in forests, and they were involved in kidnapping people, including children. They used children as baits in traps set for lions and tigers in the forest. When they caught a lion or a tiger, they would trade the skin with rifles from imperial Ethiopia. They also kidnapped those Anywaa who were traveling by themselves and traded them as slaves with the Gaala for rifles or food. There is a small tribe that borders the Anywaa people called Opwo. This tribe was intensively raided by both the Anywaa and Gaala. The Anywaa raided Opwo so they could exchange them for rifles with the Gaala. Thus, the Anywaa referred to the Opwo with a derogatory word: *Langngo*.[8] *Langngo* is an Anywaa word for slave. The Anywaa organized political and military structure prevented them from the devastating slave activities during the Abyssinian empire.

---

6. Zewde, "Relations Between Ethiopia and Sudan," 55.
7. Perner, *Why Did You Come If You Leave Again*, 60.
8. Kurimoto, "Natives and Outsiders," 6.

Slavery under Imperial Ethiopia

In 1906, three European powers (British, France, and Italy) signed a tripartite treaty which contained two things: it defined their interest and laid down guidelines for future colonial activity in the Abyssinian Empire.[9] By 1922, the Abyssinian empire received tremendous pressure from these three powers, suggesting that the only way to wipe out slavery in Ethiopia was if they (the three powers) controlled and policed their respective areas.[10] These imperialist powers used slavery activities in Ethiopia to find a way to invade Ethiopia. Bahru Zewde stated:

> First, some administrative measures were suggested to check the slave trade. One of these measures was Sudan government administration of the Anywaa plains, although the Anywaa were not subjected to the same degree of devastating slaving activities as the people of Gimira and Maji to the south and southeast.[11]

Even though the Ethiopian state had started making progress on getting rid of slavery in the 1920s, the fear of invasion by the European powers gave Ethiopia no choice but to show their progress on abolishing slavery. In order to keep their independence and get accepted into the League of Nations, Ethiopia needed to abolish slavery and present itself as a civilized country (according to what the Europeans considered as a civilized country at that time). The abolishment of slavery was one of the things that Ethiopia needed to do to join the League of Nations. Tafari (who later became Hiale Selassie) proclaimed edicts against slavery and the slave trade, which allowed his country to join the League of Nations in 1923. On October 3, 1935, Mussolini of Italy invaded Abyssinia and took over Addis Ababa after defeating emperor Haile Selassie in May of 1936. Emperor Haile Selassie left Ethiopia and went into exile. Even though it is not documented anywhere, the Anywaa people believed that emperor Haile Selassie used the port in Gambella to escape to Sudan, which gave him way out of Ethiopia.

After emperor Haile Selassie left the country, the Italians took over Gambella in 1936. When the anthropologist Evans-Pritchard was commissioned in the Sudan Defence Force in 1940, he recruited Anywaa soldiers from Anywaa country and fought against the Italians army. In his book, Clifford Geertz (the Anywaa called him Odier wa Cang) described the Anywaa fighters as follows:

9. Iadarola, "Ethiopia's Admission," 601–22.
10. Iadarola, "Ethiopia's Admission," 601–22.
11. Zewde, "Relations Between Ethiopia and the Sudan," 50.

> I may say here something of the qualities of the Anuak as fighters. They are brave, but become very excited and expose themselves unnecessarily. They like to fire from the hip and when firing from the shoulder do not use the sights, so to conduct a successful skirmish it is necessary to take them right up to the enemy and let them shoot at point-blank range.[12]

The Anywaa fighters played a big role in clearing the Italian invaders out of the Anywaa country by consistently attacking Italian forces. The Anywaa did not like the Italians even though the Italians tried to recruit some of them into their irregular bands using gifts such as clothes and food. Even though Ethiopia came under the Italian occupation, the Italians faced great resistance in the Anywaa country and other parts of Ethiopia as well. When Haile Selassie returned to Ethiopia from exile, he officially abolished slavery in Ethiopia on the August 26, 1942. This proclamation made slavery illegal in Ethiopia and imposed serious consequences for anyone who violated it.

This dark history during the Abyssinian Empire left a stigma that still affects dark-skinned people in Ethiopia today. If you are a dark-skinned person from Gambella or the Benishangul-Gumuz region and you walk in the streets of Addis Ababa today, you are likely to be called, in a derogatory way, *bariya* or *shanqella*, meaning "slave" or "dark" respectively. In the Gambella region, the words *bariya* or *shanqella* are not openly used by anyone. But colorism and discrimination in Ethiopia show their visibility by the time you step outside of Gambella. The indigenous of Gambella are Nilotic (the majority of Gambella), but there is a big population of highlanders (light-skinned people) in Gambella, where they live peacefully without being discriminated against. They are involved in the regional economy and work in different fields of their profession without any discrimination against them. Skin color is not an issue in Gambella unless there is a conflict between Gambellans and highlanders. This is the only time when skin color plays a role. For instance, when a Gambellan gets into a fight with a highlander, the federal forces (mainly highlanders) will discriminatorily side with the highlanders and abuse the Gambellan. The colorism and discrimination that dark-skinned people face in Addis Ababa and some universities in different regions are also clearly tied to the dark history of Ethiopia which most Ethiopians ignore and hide from the world.

Another word that is widely used in a derogatory way in Ethiopia to refer to dark skinned people from Gambella as slaves is *Lemma*. This

12. Geertz, "Works and Lives," 54.

name came from the name of a military general under the Emperor Haile Selassie. General Lemma was an imperial governor of Gambella who was appointed by the central government in the 1960s. General Lemma was an Amhara by ethnicity. According to Dereje Feyissa, General Lemma was sent to Gambella because of his involvement in the failed 1960 coup that was orchestrated against Emperor Haile Selassie.[13] So, appointing him as a governor of Gambella was a sort of punishment and a form of exclusion. Furthermore, his assignment as a governor of Gambella put him under the leadership of Enquselassie (the governor of Illubabor province), which was his rival at that time. As a result of the General Lemma governing Gambella, the indigenous people of Gambella were labeled the "People of Lemma" by the central government. This labeling made General Lemma look as if he were a slave master that owned the dark-skinned people of Gambella, not a governor. Today, the name *Lemma* is derogatorily used by some light-skinned Ethiopians to refer to Gambella people as the slaves of General Lemma.

The colorism and discrimination in Ethiopia against dark-skinned people is institutionalized and purposefully left unaddressed. Thus, skin color became some kind of scale that is used to weigh whether someone is more or less Ethiopian. For instance, if a Gambellan speaks fluent Amharic in a taxi in Addis Ababa, they will be looked at with curiosity and a shocked facial expression for speaking the official language of Ethiopia. If you are not light-skinned, just like the majority of Ethiopia, you will be automatically seen or treated like foreigners. It is common in Addis Ababa for most Gambellans to be asked how come they can speak Amharic, which is the working language of the federal government and the Gambella region. The colorism that Gambella people face in Ethiopia has led to the point where a Gambellan person must be accompanied by their light-skinned friends when looking for a rental property or purchasing something in Addis Ababa; the price will be doubled or higher if they're by themselves. Being called *Lemma*, *bariya*, or *shankella* is a norm for dark-skinned Ethiopians. It is even worse that the dark-skinned Ethiopians are also sometimes being insulted and referred to as monkeys, *keseli* (meaning charcoal), or *goma* (meaning tire) in their own country. These words are intentionally used in a very racist and discriminatory way against Gambellan, Benishangul-Gumuz, and other Nilotic Ethiopians.

---

13. Dereje, *Playing Different Games*, 126.

This colorism and discrimination in Ethiopia against the Gambellans is also systemic and incorporated within the central government. Gambella is currently one of the poorest or least developed regions in Ethiopia. The people of Gambella, mainly the Anywaa people, were denied education, healthcare, clean water, and other necessities for humans. The Anywaa people never had access to education until Emperor Haile Selassie returned to Ethiopia from exile in 1941. The first school in Gambella was opened in 1942, the same year that slavery was officially abolished by the Emperor Haile Selassie. When the first American missionaries reached the Anywaa people, they opened a primary school in Akobo (on the Sudan side) in 1940–50. American missionaries built the first school in Akado village (on the Ethiopia side) in 1952. This school was much better and better-equipped than the school that was built by Emperor Haile Selassie. Before building a school for the Anywaa people, the missionaries were told by the emperor to only open the school from first through third grade. This was to prevent the Anywaa people from having a higher education. However, third grade education wasn't enough for Anywaa to be able to help with Bible translation. Don McClure asked the emperor for a favor again, and he was allowed to extend the classes to sixth grade only. The second school was then opened by the American Presbyterian Church in Gilo village in 1960. Despite being in Ethiopia, the Anywaa people's access to education was limited to sixth grade during the Emperor Haile Selassie. This was a part of the discrimination against the Anywaa people embedded within the Ethiopian government. The Anywaa people were not also fully acknowledged as Ethiopian citizens even though the Ethiopian police were present in Gambella.

Every year, all Ethiopians from the four corners of Ethiopia and Africans celebrate the victory of Ethiopia against Italy at the battle of Adwa on March 1, 1896. This war was fought by the people under imperial Ethiopia including the allies such as the Anywaa people who had trade relationships and also faced the same aggression from the colonizers (the British) from the Sudan side and Italians in Gambella. After the defeat of the Italians, one of the people who was awarded by King Menelik II was an Anywaa warrior named Oballa Nyigwo from Gambella. He was presented with a sword from Emperor Menelik II. The victory of Adwa was a victory of Black people, and it brings pride not only to Ethiopians but to all Africans. During the battle, all Ethiopians paid the price and sacrificed for their freedom: the dark-skinned people, lighter-skinned people, the rich, the poor, and all

Ethiopians from different ethnicities. Yet, Black-on-Black slavery continued to be practiced throughout the Abyssinian Empire even after the defeat of the Italians. Imperial Ethiopia became one of the two African nations free of European colonization, but it continued to enslave and oppress its fellow Africans. Despite the discrimination and colorism against the Anywaa people, they tremendously continued to sacrifice for Ethiopia during the second invasion of Italy in 1935. During the Korean War (1950–53), Ethiopia participated and fought as a part of the American-led UN troops to support South Korea against communist North Korea. This made Ethiopia the only African country and non-NATO member to participate in the Korean War. The Anywaa people represented Ethiopia and fought in the Korean War. The Anywaa heroes like Ojwanga Gilo fought in the Korean war, but he was never acknowledged by any Ethiopian leaders except until Prime Minister Dr. Abiy Ahmed Ali, PhD, came to power in 2018. During his visit to Gambella on May 20, 2018, Prime Minister Abiy gave a speech in Gambella Stadium and publicly acknowledged the Anywaa heroes like Ojwanga Gilo who fought on behalf of his country Ethiopia during the Korean War. But, the Anywaa people remember Ojwanga Gilo as the person who killed Gallas (the Anywaa use the word to refer to all the highlanders) police in Addis Ababa. In their *agwaga* song, the Anywaa people recorded the incident where they would repeatedly sing the phrase "Ojwanga killed the Gallas."

Chapter 4

American Missionaries to the Anywaa People

HARVEY HOEKSTRA (ODOLA OTOURA) and Don McClure (Odan) were the first missionaries to reach the Anywaa people. Rev. William Donald McClure or Odan (the name given to him by the Anywaa people) was born in Blairsville, Pennsylvania, to his mother Margaret McNaughter and father Robert Elmer McClure. After finishing his college from Westminster College in Pennsylvania, Don decided to go to the Anglo-Egyptian Sudan and volunteered in a mission school. This was the first time he was exposed to the Anywaa and Shilluk (Chollo) Luo group. When he returned to the United States, Don went to Pittsburgh-Xenia Seminary and returned to Sudan where he worked at Doleib Hill with the support of the United Presbyterian Church. He and his wife Leyda McClure dedicated their life to serving the Shilluk before he started the Anywaa Project. In one of the letters he wrote from Pokwo, Don McClure described the Anywaa people as "godless" people. However, before the Anywaa heard about Jesus and Christianity, they believed that there is a god that is above everything and the creator of all things and its name is *Jwok or Chuway*. They also believed that there are two kinds of gods (juu, the plural for jwok): *Jwok-Nyingolabwuo* and *Jwok-Nyoodungo*. *Jwok-Nyingolabwuo* is believed by the Anywaa people as a good god who protects people from harm. The Anywaa also believed that *Jwok-Nyingolabwuo* brings rain for people to farm and drives away diseases from the community. While *jwok-nyoodungo* is considered a bad or evil god who brings diseases, famines, draughts, and crises to the community. *Jwok-nyoodungo* also could possess a tree, rock, or live in a pool or a river. It demands sacrifices from people, and if not provided, the Anywaa believed that it would kill or bring a terrible disease to the people. When there is a pregnant woman in the village, this *jwok-nyoodungo* would sometimes ask the mother or the owner of the land to name the child after its name. If the parents refused, the Anywaa believed that it would kill the child or the child would be disabled when it is born. Most of these gods live in the rivers, and the rivers or pools are named after them. Some of the names such as Kiiru, Aballa, Cham, Nyingori, Thatha, Oleng, Nyimulu, and Dingur are named after these gods. When the Anywaa people received the gospel of Jesus, many of them converted within a short period of time. The Anywaa project was sponsored by Don's American denomination in 1937 and donated $1,000 for the initiation of the project in Akobo (1938–50).[1] According to Partee, the goal of the Anywaa project was to plant and nourish a Christian church among the Anywaae, which involved translating the Bible into Dha-Anywaa.[2]

Harvey Hoekstra or Odola Otoura (the name given to him by the Anywaa people) was appointed by Don McClure to translate the New Testament into Dha-Anywaa. The first Bible in Dha-Anywaa was written in Latin and completed in 1961. There were very important people who played a great role in completing and reviewing the very first Bible in Dha-Anywaa. The people included Othow wera Adier, Ezekiel Ochala Lero, James Buya, pastor Akway Ochudho, Okac Ojwato, Stephen Omod, Dr. James Keefer (the name given to him by Anywaae is Oman Cham), and Rev. Niles Reimer or Okwomchor (name given to him by Anywaae). In his writing, Harvey Hoekstra stated:

> The team that worked together longest and to the completion of the translation were Ezekiel Ochala Alero and Othow war Adier. Ezekiel had 8 years of schooling. His English was quite good and improved appreciably with added years. Othow was an intelligent member of the team and I was deeply grateful for him. He knew no English, and was unschooled but a man whose judgment I greatly respected. I had him on the team because I wanted someone who knew no English. This forced us to speak in Anywaa as we discussed each verse before transcribing it on a 3 x 5 file paper.

---

1. Partee, *Adventure in Africa*, loc. 2542.

2. Dha-Anywaa is the language that Anywaa people speak. Sometimes it is written as "Anuak language" or "Anywaa language."

In a sense, Othow had to be satisfied that the translation was saying it the way Anywaaks thought and spoke.[3]

When the Italians invaded Ethiopia in 1935, the war spread and prevented Don McClure from doing his mission in Akobo. The Sudan government refused to have him returned to the Anywaa people, and they had to stay at Doleib Hill serving the Shilluk. When the war was over in 1941, Don McClure was able to help emperor Haile Selassie in Khartoum when his car broke down. Don took him to his appointment, and this gesture of kindness would serve Don in the long run. When Don McClure returned to Akobo and resumed his missionary work, he built the first school for the Anywaa people. According to Partee, Don McClure received a great number of students that he could not handle.[4] He stated that forty boys walked for more than a hundred miles to get to school, so he couldn't send them back home but to enroll them. This was a clear indication of how thirsty the Anywaa people were for the school, which was just introduced to them by the American missionaries for the very first time. After serving the Anywaa of Akobo for years, Don McClure decided to go deeper into the Anywaa land in Gambella, Ethiopia, in 1950.

When Don McClure arrived in Ethiopia, he had a meeting with the emperor Haile Selassie in his palace in Addis Ababa. During that meeting, Don reminded the king of how he helped him in Khartoum when his car broke down and presented him with the proposal of the Anywaa project in Ethiopia. According to Don McClure, the king responded in Amharic, and it was translated by Tafara Worq, saying:

> I want to thank you for coming, and I want to thank your mission and your board in America for understanding this work among the Anuak. I am deeply interested in these people of the lowlands and want to learn more about them. I will grant you immediate permission to open this work among the Anuak people in Ethiopia. When can you start?"[5]

The emperor Haile Selassie gave Don McClure permission to reach the Anywaa people because he also wanted to learn and get information about the Anywaa people. One of the things that Don McClure highlighted during this meeting was hearing the king referring to the Anywaa people as

---

3. "History of the Translation."
4. Partee, *Adventure in Africa*, loc. 3785
5. Partee, *Adventure in Africa*, loc. 4413

"my people," which was different from the word *shanqalla* that people used to refer to the Anywaa at that time. King Haile Selassie also gave permission to Don McClure to teach the Anywaa people in Dha-Anywaa and offered help to provide Amharic books and teachers at his expense when the Anywaa people became ready to learn the official Ethiopian language.[6]

Don McClure started his missionary work in Pokwo where he shared the gospel and also opened a little clinic under a tree. Just like they had done in Akobo, having a clinic to treat the sick people was an effective way of sharing the gospel with the patients. Even though Don McClure and his wife Lyda were not physicians, they tried their best to help the Anywaa people as there was no hospital available for the Anywaa people in Pokwo. He didn't know what he was doing most of the time, but he trusted the lord with it. As he stated:

> I gave out hundreds of pills, some of which I knew what they were good for (such as aspirin and cascara), and some I did not (such as Erythrocin-Neomycin). On the other hand, I did not know what disease I was treating half the time either. So, I assume everything balanced out.[7]

During this time, the governor of Gambella was *Kenyasmach* Asfau Abejie and he was appointed by emperor Haile Selassie. The Anywaa people still had no access to good healthcare until Don McClure opened one in Pokwo. Hundreds of Anywaa people from closer villages and many miles away had to walk to Pokwo to get help that the American missionaries could provide. Don McClure gave the Anywaa people access not only to school but also healthcare which was much better than the traditional witch doctor practices that the Anywaa had depended on for generations. He also kept his relationship in good shape with Emperor Haile Selassie by providing the information asked by the emperor about the Anywaa people. In his letter, Don McClure expressed how he was questioned a lot about the Anywaa people by Tafara Worq and the emperor Hiale Selassie. Don became a source for the Abyssinian empire to obtain information about the Anywaa political system, customs, populations, and many other things.

The Anywaa people started fighting the Ethiopian police located in Gambella after the Ethiopian Ministry of Education made it mandatory to only teach in Amharic throughout the country. The school in Pokwo

6. Partee, *Adventure in Africa*, loc. 4439
7. Partee, *Adventure in Africa*, loc. 5079

was closed down as a result of this mandate, which angered the Anywaa people. This was the time when people of Pokumo attacked and defeated the Ethiopian police, ceasing their weapons, including a machine gun. When the Ethiopian police reorganized for revenge months later, they were ambushed and defeated again by the people of Pokumo.[8] In his letter about his meeting with king Haile Selassie, Don McClure said:

> I also pointed out that the Anuaks had become resentful of the imperial government and of us for refusing to teach them in their own language. Moreover, the Anuak people can never be made good citizens of Ethiopia by force.[9]

Closing the school in Pokwo was seen by the Anywaa people as denial of access to education. Thus, they use force to protest the involvement of king Haile Selassie in their affair. They were not happy with the presence and movement of Ethiopian police on their land, and mandated them to learn in Amharic language, which they considered a "foreign language." Don McClure served the Anywaa people in Akobo, Sudan (1938–50), Pokwo, Ethiopia (1950–60), and Gilo, Ethiopia (1960–62). Then he served in Addis Ababa and Gode, Ethiopia. Don McClure was killed in Gode by Somali guerrillas in 1977 and was buried by his son Don Jr. at the mission site in Gode under a large tree.[10]

The New Testament that was fully translated into Dha-Anywaa by Odola (Harvey Hoekstra) reached Pokwo, Ethiopia, in 1962. The emperor Haile Selassie permitted the Anywaa people to read the Bible in their language. However, the government didn't want the Bible to be written in Latin. Therefore, the Anywaa Bible had to be transliterated into Amharic script. The people who worked to transliterate the Anywaa Bible from Latin to Amharic script in Pokwo included Dr. Jim Keefer (Oman Cham), Ato Isaac Omod Okon, and Qes Okac Ojwato. Even though the Anywaa had their New Testament Bible in their own language, the Old Testament was

---

8. Though the Ethiopian police suffered a great lost in Pokumo, they burned down small villages and farms in Baat-Openo area and killed civilians, which forced farmers, women, and children to flee to other villages, causing mass displacement.

9. Partee, *Adventure in Africa*, loc. 5580

10. Don McClure Jr. moved to Gambella after he finished his school and served the Nuer refugees who were fleeing the civil war in Sudan. Don Jr. brought thousands of Nuer refugees to the heart of the Anywaa land and placed them in a new camp called Kadesh in Baat-Openo. This camp was named by one of the Nuer refugees, referring to the Kadesh in the Bible that the Israelites camped at on their way to Canaan (the promised land).

not fully translated at that time. In 1955, a missionary named Rev. Niles Reimer (the Anywaa called him Okwomchor) and his wife Ann (Dickason) Reimer (the Anywaa called her Nyodier) went to Pokwo, Ethiopia, and served as Presbyterian missionaries. They were accompanied by a twenty-three-year-old young nurse named Marie (Breezy) Lusted; the Anywaa people called her Nyajaak. Nyajaak served as a nurse at Pokwo clinic and helped with proofreading the Anywaa Bible that was transliterated into Ethiopic Fidel. These American Presbyterian missionaries served the Anywaa people at Pokwo Station and worked on translating the rest of the Bible into Dha-Anywaa.

When the Anywaa people asked about who would translate the rest of the Bible into Dha-Anywaa, Nyajaak offered to work on it. When they started their work, they had to translate both with the Ethiopic Fidel for the Anywaa people in Ethiopia, and in Latin for those in Sudan. Philip Omod Daw made rough drafts in Ethiopic Fidel, and Isaac Omod Okon reviewed the drafts along with Nyajaak.[11] This tiring and time-consuming task of translation was taken on by this group while Nyajaak was also working in the Pokwo clinic. The village of Pokwo resembled its name, which is translated as "the village of life." The Anywaa people walked for miles to get help in Pokwo Clinic, which was fully run by the American missionaries. While serving the Anywaa people in Pokwo, Rev. Niles Reimer (Okwomchor) and Ann Reimer lost their child in 1973. Their daughter's name was Beth Reimer, and she was only eight years old when she was bitten by a rat. Beth was buried in Pokwo, Ethiopia. When the Derg government took power in Ethiopia, the American Missionaries moved to Addis Ababa. The Anywaa people who contributed to the translation of the Anywaa Bible in Addis Ababa were Omod Ochan, Mamo Oman, Okwier Oletho, Okello Akway, Omod Agwa, Thwol Omod, Omod Ongom, Ojulu Cham, Paul Othow, Ajulu Ojwato, and Desalegn Omod.[12] There were also many people who dedicated their time and energy to reviewing the translated books, making sure that the translations were accurate and had good quality. Among those who played a big role were Kes Akway Ochudho, Kes Aba Okeng, Kes Ojulu Nyang, Kes Ochala Abula, Kes Okach Ojwato, Isaac Omod Okon, John Aciek Omod, Nyidieri Oliiri, and Apiew Kweth. Those people made sure that the translations were good, a tiring job that required meetings, discussions, readings, and correcting anything that needed to be corrected.

11. "History of the Translation."
12. "History of the Translation."

The Anywaa Bible translation was completed in 2010, and it was sent to the publisher. After the Bible was completed, it was sent to Korea for printing. The Anywaa people in Gambella, Ethiopia, finally received the whole Bible in Dha-Anywaa (Old and New Testament) on April 11, 2013.

The Anywaa people came from all over the world and celebrated the dedication of the full Anywaa Bible in Gambella Mekane Yesus Bethel Synop on July 6, 2013. Thousands of Anywaa people gathered in Mekane Yesus compound to celebrate the completion of the Anywaa Bible. Okwomchor and his wife Nyodier and a team from the United States were present in-person. Nyajaak was not able to go to Gambella due to health issues, but she joined on Skype to share the joys of this historical moment with the Anywaa people. They served the lord with all their hearts, energy, and time, and finished the work of the lord for the Anywaa people. They sacrificed all they had, dedicated their entire lives to serving the Anywaa people, and translated the Bible into Dha-Anywaa. This is something that the Anywaa people will remember for all the generations to come. After finishing the work of the Lord, Okwomchor, Nyodier, and Nyajaak went to the lord. Nyodier or Ann Reimer passed away and went to the Lord on August 14, 2016, in Denver, Colorado, at age 85. On October 29, 2017, in North Carolina, Nyajaak or Marie "Breezy" Lusted went to the Lord at the age of 85. Okwomchor or Rev. Nile Reimer went to Lord Jesus Christ on December 21, 2019 in Greeley, Colorado, at the age of 92. They are with the Lord today, and the Anywaa people have the word of God in their hands.

PART 2

Chapter 5

Anywaa under the Communist Derg Regime

When the Derg regime overthrew king Haile Selassie in 1974, Mengistu Haile Mariam abolished the monarchy in Ethiopia and replaced it with a socialist government. This change also reached the Anywaa people, who were historically ruled by kings and chiefs. The Derg government destroyed the monarchy and chiefdom of the Anywaa people in Gambella and replaced them with government agents. He also tried to destroy and replace some of the things in Anywaa tradition which he considered as bad traditions or backwards practices. One of the practices that the Derg government tried to destroy was the use of *dimuuy (dimui)* as a means of currency. *Dimuuy* is a very important and rare bead in the Anywaa tradition. Due to its scarcity, *Dimuuy* is considered as the most valuable bead that a person can own. Those with possession of *Dimuuye* (plural) are viewed as wealthy or people with higher status in the community. This rare bead is used for multiple purposes. For instance, if someone commits a serious crime such as murder, *dimuuy* would be used to pay the family of the deceased as compensation. It is up to the victim's family to demand how many *dimuuye* they would want. *Dimuuy* is also used for marriage dowries. For a young Anywaa man to get married, he would need to have *dimuuy* to give to the family of the woman as a dowry or bride price. So, it is essential to have *dimuuy* as an Anywaa man. Families with many girls/women usually don't lack *dimuuye* compared to families with only boys/men. This demand for *dimuuy* had forced the Anywaa men with no sisters to go to places like

Dambala[1] to mine gold. Some people went to Oromia to work in the coffee fields. Once they earned enough money, they would go back to Gambella and buy *dimuuye*, which would help them to pay dowries.

During the Derg government, *dimuuye* were forcefully collected by the Derg militia and had them burned. Some of them were thrown into the rivers or taken away by the militias, which the Anywaa people viewed as an attempt to destroy the culture and tradition. In many Anywaa villages, the Derg militia would go from home to home searching for the beads and burn them. This forced the Anywaa people to hide the *dimuuye* and other important beads by burying them down or running away with them. The main purpose of destroying *dimuuy* was to introduce a new way of transaction to the Anywaa people, which was using paper currency. There were also other things in the Anywaa tradition that the Derg government forbade such as *naak* and *otak*. *Naak* is an Anywaa cultural practice which involves the removal of lower front teeth. This was viewed as a sign of beauty specifically for the women. *Otak* was a tradition mainly practiced in marriage. It was used as a way of punishing a man who denies being the father after impregnating a woman, those who abuse their wives, and anyone who commits adultery. The Derg government viewed this as a harmful and backwards traditional practice and tried to prohibit it. But the Anywaa people viewed the move as an attempt to destroy their ways of life. There were some other practices that the Derg government prohibited, which many Anywaa people today praised it for. For instance, the Derg government prohibited drinking alcohol for people under the age of eighteen. The Anywaa people didn't see any problem with young teenagers drinking alcohol. This was because the alcohol that the Anywaa people had before the highlanders introduced an addictive *arake* was not very strong. They mostly drank *ogooli*, which was a fermented honey; *wachatha*, which is made with corn flour fermented for three days and mixed with honey after fermentation; and *boordhi* and *achota (olangngo)*, which goes through the same process. These kinds of alcohols were not very strong, and some could be considered as juice. *Kade* and *biel* were also prohibited. *Kade* is tattooing or marking the skin, which was viewed as a sign of beauty just like *Naak*. But *biel* is when a family forces a woman or little girl into a marriage with someone who is rich in exchange for money or *dimuuye*. This was one

---

1. *Dambala* is a village in Dimma woreda (one of the Anywaa woredas). This place is known for gold mining, and many people go to the area for this specific reason. The Anywaa women also go to Dambala for business purposes such as selling food and drinks to the men who are doing traditional mining.

of the practices prohibited by the Derg that the Anywaa people happily embraced, especially the Anywaa women.

The biggest transformation that the Derg government carried out in the Anywaa land was the demolition of kingship and headmanship that the Anywaa people had practiced for centuries. Many well-known scholars including C. A. Diop (1974) and Henri Frunkfort (1948) wrote about the origin of the Luo people, strongly believing that the Luo originated in Egypt. Before migrating to East and Central Africa, the Luo people are believed to be the founders and builders of the ancient Koch or Cushitic kingdom at Napata. The well-organized structure of the Anywaa political system ties them to their ancient early civilization. It is not clear when the Anywaa people started governing themselves using a monarchical political system. Even though there are no written documents about the origin of the Anywaa's two political systems (*kwar* and *nyec*), Anywaa oral stories show that the first political system that the Anywaa people used to rule themselves was *kwar* or chiefdom. The first Anywaa chief to lead the Anywaa people is believed to be Kwaaro (chief) Cwaay (Cheway, Chwai)[2]. The exact date when Kwaaro Cwaay created the early chiefdom political system remains unknown. Kwaaro Cwaay created the structure of the *kwar*, and he ruled the Anywaa people until the first Anywaa king introduced *nyec*.

The first king to rule the Anywaa people was King Gilo o Kori. Gilo was the son of Kori, who was the daughter of Cwaay. Ochudho was brought to the village of Cwaay after he made a fair judgment and settled a dispute over fish between two boys. The two boys caught a fish from the river; one of them held it by the head and the other by the tail. When Ochudho saw the two boys quarreling, he told the boy who was holding the fish by its head to stop holding the fish. When the boy stopped holding the fish by its head, the fish slipped through and went back to the river. When the two boys went back to fishing, they both caught a fish again; one was holding the head, and the other was holding the tail. Ochudho told the boy who was holding the fish by its tail to let it go. This time the fish didn't slip away, and the boy who was holding the fish by its head took the fish. Then, Ochudho told them that the person who holds the fish by its head owns the fish. The boys were impressed by his wise judgment, and they went back to the village and told Chief Cwaay about what happened. Then, Cwaay sent his men to the river to capture Ochudho. The name of the river that Ochudho was

---

2. *Cwaay* literally means "creator" in English.

captured from was Pul Amai (Evans-Pritchard, 1940).[3] Kori, the daughter of Cwaay, was impregnated by Ochudho when she was appointed to take care of him after he was captured and brought to the village.

After impregnating Kori, Ochudho escaped and returned to the river. Ochudho left the bead *ocwok* that he was wearing to Kori before leaving, and the beads became an emblem for *nyec* or kingship. When Kori gave birth to her son, the child was named Gilo. The name Gilo came from the Anywaa word *gillo*, which is a disease that enlarges or swells the stomach. This was because Kori lied to her father Cwaay that she was not pregnant but sick. When Gilo was born, he was raised by his mother and uncles from his mother's side. That's why in the Anywaa tradition, the maternal uncles play a big role in appointing their nephew as a new king. Gilo became the first king in Anywaa society. Though there is no record of the kingship establishment in Anywaa society, this mythical story about the origin of kingship was orally passed on through generations. The Anywaa people believe that kings come from the river because Ochudho was captured by the river. This is the reason when a king dies, the Anywaa refer to it as "*Nyeya adoo naam*," meaning "the king has returned to the river." The demolition of kingdomship and chiefdom by the Derg regime initiated the fall and destruction of the Anywaa society since their society is built around kingship and chiefdom.

---

3. Evans-Pritchard, *Political System*, 78.

Anywaa under the Communist Derg Regime

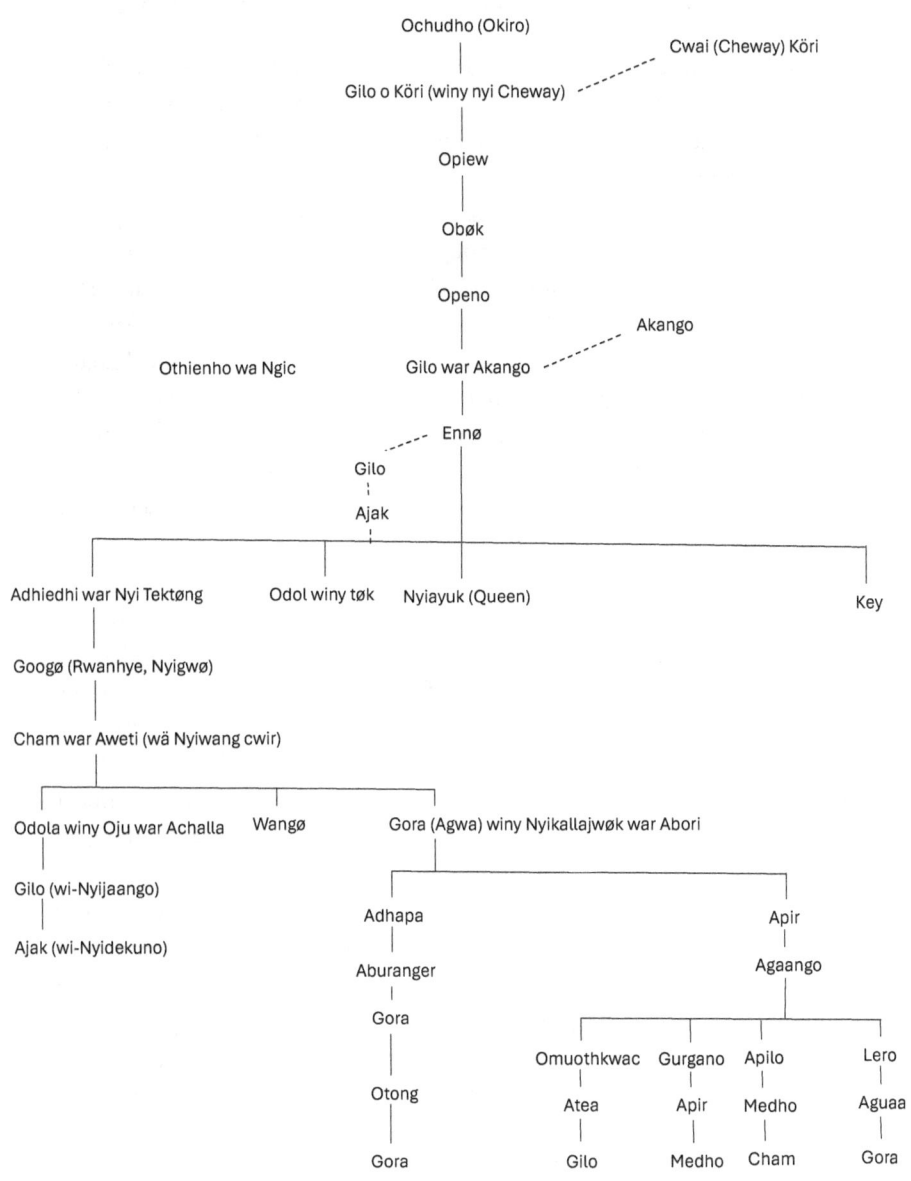

The Anywaa royal genealogy.[4]

---

4. Reconstructed from Evans-Pritchard, *Political System of the Anuak*; Perner, *Living on Earth in the Sky*, 82–84.

The Impact of Highlander Settlers on the Anywaa People

In 1984, the first settlers arrived in Gambella from three different provinces in Ethiopia: Tigrayans from Tigray province, Amhara from Wollo province, and Kambata from Gamo Gofa province.[5] More than sixty thousand settlers were brought to Gambella and settled in thirty-four settlement areas (*menders*)[6] in the Anywaa lands. *Menders* one through six were placed in the Baat-Openo area; seven through twenty-five in the Abwobo area; twenty-six through thirty-four in the Gog and Jor area. Prior to the Sudanese second civil war and the highlander settlers in the 1980s, the Anywaa people had the largest population in Gambella, followed by the Majang people. However, the 1984 settlement program drastically changed the demographic of Gambella. According to Cultural Survival, there were plans outlined under the direction of the United States to develop the Anywaa's rich lands, and the final proposal was submitted to the European Economic Commission (EEC) in 1978.[7]

However, the Derg government requested the EEC to transfer the funds allocated to the Baro scheme to another project. This project was the resettlement of highlanders in the Anywaa lands. This project included the construction of dams, clearing of lands for agriculture, displacement of the Anywaa people from their ancestral lands, building fences and barriers to keep wild animals from the farms, building schools for the new settlers, and construction of roads for transportation. Roads were built to connect Gambella to other regions in Ethiopia and to connect Gambella town to Itang, Jikaw, Abwobo, and Pinyudo (Pignudo).[8]

The Derg government gathered students from different universities in Ethiopia and sent them to Gambella to prepare the *menders* and built huts for the settlers. The students were involved in gathering wood and grass for construction and building huts. Even though Derg government claimed that the goal of this resettlement program was for relief due to the famine in Tigray and Wello, it was criticized because the real purpose was

---

5. Kurimoto, "Multidimensional Impact," 5.

6. *Mender* is an Amharic word for a village. Most of the settlers died due to malaria in the Gambella region. Due to lack of thorough study of the land and locations, most *menders* were destroyed by floods during the rainy season, and they were closed. The only successful *menders* were the ones located in Abwobo woreda.

7. "Anuak Displacement and Ethiopian Resettlement."

8. Kurimoto, "Multidimensional Impact," 4.

to depopulate the strongholds of the rebel movement.[9] But one thing that the Anywaa people believed that the Derg government was trying to do was to change the demography of Gambella and mix the Nilotic Anywaa with the highlanders. During my interview with Willie Gilo Lumson, he said:

> The Derg government wanted the Anywaa people to intermarry with the settlers so that the majority of Gambella people would have lighter skin, which is what they [majority ethnicities in Ethiopia] think Ethiopians should look like.[10]

Cultural Survival reported that the Anywaa people were forcefully ordered to evacuate two neighborhoods in Gambella called Betourhe and Ajumara in 1984. Then the Ethiopian government built houses for the Soviet specialists who were sent at that time to work on a dam and irrigation scheme. When the Alworo Dam was built in 1985 by the Soviet specialists, the Anywaa people were forced to relocate from the old Abwobo town into a new location, today's Abwobo. The Anywaa had to leave behind their farms, which they inherited from their ancestors and were intergenerationally passed on to them. Willie Gilo Lumson said:

> The people of Abwobo were not supported with the relocation process. They were just told to leave behind their houses, farms and start from scratch in a totally new environment without any help from the government.[11]

Those Soviet specialists from Russia were not only involved in construction but also mining natural resources without the knowledge of the local Anywaa community. It was mainly in the Abwobo and Pinyudo area, where they were digging large pits in the forest, leaving the uneducated Anywaa community wondering what the white men were doing at night. One of the things that fueled anger with the Derg regime in the Anywaa community was the closing of the American missionary schools in 1985. The Anywaa people responded with anger just like they did when the Emperor Haile Selassie closed the missionaries' schools in Gambella because of the new rule that demanded that all schools in Ethiopia teach in Amharic. According to Cultural Survival, the Derg government closed the schools in Gambella so that the students and teachers could cut down wood and grass and erect

---

9. Kurimoto, "Multidimensional Impact," 5.
10. Interview with Willie Gilo Lumson (January 18, 2021).
11. Interview with Willie Gilo Lumson (January 18, 2021).

huts in the camp.[12] This also was the time when the Ethiopian government expelled US missionaries who were teaching the Anywaa and giving them educational opportunities at that time. The Anywaa people were not happy with this expulsion because they considered it a systematic denial of the right to achieve higher education, and a way to keep the Anywaa people illiterate.

As a result of the resettlement program, the Anywaa people were forced to leave their farms and integrated into the new *menders* with the highlanders, who were three times larger in population than the local Anywaa people. When those thousands of settlers (highlanders) settled in the Anywaa lands, it resulted in mass deforestation which exponentially decreased the forests in Anywaa lands. It also increased the crime rates, which made it very hard for the Anywaa people to freely travel from one place to another like they used to. The arrival of new settlers also introduced a new strong *araki* (alcohol) to the Anywaa people, which led to addiction and a great alcoholism issue in the region. This new alcohol caused a lack of work habits, and most farms went without being farmed. Furthermore, the numbers of new babies declined as the alcohol took hold of the Anywaa community. Resources also became scarce and mass emigration of animals occurred, specifically the elephants, giraffes, hippopotamuses, and other wild animals became rare to find in Gambella. The Anywaa people are hunters, and they get their protein diets mostly from the wild animals such as wild boar, deer, buffalo, and many other wild animals in Gambella. The population of fish species also decreased because of this resettlement program. According to Cultural Survival, in 1984 the government forced the Anywaa farmers living in Okuna Kejang in the Abwobo district to integrate in the southern hall Illubabor.[13] When the Anywaa refused to leave, the government brought tractors and plowed the riverbank crops to starve the Anywaa people who refused to leave their ancestral land. This led to the Anywaa fleeing the area, and the government used these areas for the settlers. As a result, the Anywaa people lost their economic power and became dependent on the highlanders for food. Willie Gilo Lumson stated that the resettlement program was meant to open a way for intermarry with the Anywaa people and mix them with the lighter-skinned highlanders to eliminate the darker-skinned Anywaa people, which was a form of silent genocide. For instance, the population of the Anywaa in Okuna at that time

12. "Anuak Displacement and Ethiopian Resettlement."
13. "Anuak Displacement and Ethiopian Resettlement."

was not 10 percent of the settlers that were in that area. The Anywaa people were forced to learn the Amharic and Oromo languages. As a result, many Anywaa people became fluent in both Amharic and Oromifa language. During Sunday services, Anywaa people even started singing songs in Amharic. Willie Gilo Lumson said:

> This was a tactic to change the culture and language of the Anywaa people and introduce them to the highlanders' cultures and languages.[14]

Mr. Willie Gilo Lumson was interviewed on January 18, 2021.

14. Interview with Willie Gilo Lumson (January 18, 2021).

Chapter 6

The Refugees in Anywaa Lands

THE ANYWAA PEOPLE STARTED to feel the impact of refugees when the first civil war broke out between the northern and southern part of Sudan in 1955. The Anywaa lands in Ethiopia and part of Sudan were used by the rebel group also known as the Anya Nya I or Anyanya I (the first Southern Sudan Guerilla group in the first civil war [1955–72]). Kuyok Abol Kuyok stated that the first four people who formed the Anya Nya I rebel group were Paul Nyingori, Paul Ruot, Paul Adung, and Paul Awel. Paul Nyingori Ojulu Oloyo was an Anywaa who was born around 1936 in a place called Ajwaara, Akobo.[1] Paul joined the movement in July 1963 after he was convinced by Paul Ruot, his former schoolmate. The first place that the four Pauls approached was Pochala, Sudan, and they established the first camp of the Anya Nya I. This first camp that was established was named Dhaldiim, located in the northern part of Pochala. According to Okello Akway, when the first refugees arrived in Ethiopia, General Lemma met with the Anywaa leaders of Po-Mooli and some other villages mainly in Baat-Openo to accept the refugees who were fleeing war.[2] Then, the refugees were given places to stay until things got better in Sudan. It was also during the South Sudanese first civil war in the 1950s that the Nuer population started to settle in Gambella fleeing the civil war. The presence of Anya Nya I forces in the Anywaa's land was beneficial to the movement of the group, but the Anywaa people did not benefit. They were targeted by the Sudanese Arab

---

1. Kuyok, *South Sudan*, 422.
2. Interview with Okello Akway (August 29, 2022).

The Refugees in Anywaa Lands

government, killed, and displaced from Akobo and Nasir in suspicion of supporting the rebels. Not only were the Anya Nya I forces using the Anywaa lands as a safe haven, the Anywaa prince of Pochala provided the Anya Nya I group about 160 rifles and ammunition. According to Kuyok Abol Kuyok, Paul Nyingori was overthrown by the Anya Nya I forces in Upper Nile, and he was replaced with Cdr. Joseph Akuon.[3] In 1997, he died in Khartoum as a colonel. The first Sudanese civil war ended on February 27, 1972, after the signing of the Addis Ababa Agreement by Mansour Khalid and Joseph Lagu. The first civil war did not bring a big number of Nuer refugees to Anywaa lands in Ethiopia because most of them stayed closer to the border of the modern day of South Sudan. As a result of this war, many Anywaa villages in Akobo, Sudan, were destroyed, and people were killed and displaced from their homes by the Sudanese forces.

The second Sudanese civil war from 1983 to 2006 had caused unprecedented damage to the Anywaa people and their lands both in Sudan and Ethiopia. This is also the civil war which brought thousands of refugees to Anywaa lands in Gambella. According to Collins, on June 5, 1983, President Ja'afar Numayri went on prime-time national television and announced the dismantlement of the Addis Ababa Agreement, which led to another military insurrection.[4] On April 6, 1983, Garang founded the movement known as the Sudan People's Liberation Movement/Army (SPLM/A). This war brought hundreds of thousands of refugees to Gambella, and they greatly exceeded the local population. The Anywaa, Komo, Majang, and Opwo were the main indigenous people of Gambella. The Nuer are late comers to Gambella, but they came earlier than the settlers (highlanders).[5] Some indigenous who lived in Gambella went without being recognized by the government for a long time. For instance, Opwo[6] were not found until 1980 (1972 E.C.) when they were founded by Philip Ochudho and Agwa and the government of Ethiopia was informed about the presence of this group in Gambella. But the Nuer were not living anywhere in Gambella until the first civil war in Sudan took place. They started emigrating from Sudan (mainly Bentiu) to Anywaa lands, escaping the oppression by the

---

3. Kuyok, *South Sudan*, 372.
4. Collins, "Civil Wars in the Sudan," 1784.
5. Dereje, *Playing Different Games*, 137.
6. Opwo people are more related to the Anywaa people of Baat-Openo and Cham village. According to the former president of Gambella Okello Akway, some of the Opwo people are intermarried with the Anywaa of Baat-Openo

Arab Sudanese. During the second civil war in Sudan, the Derg regime took this opportunity to make alliance with the rebel group and invited them to Ethiopia to Anywaa lands, where he trained and armed them. On the other hand, the NIF government in Khartoum supported the Ethiopian People's Revolutionary Democratic Front (EPRDF) and Gambella People's Liberation Movement (GPLM) who were fighting Mengistu's socialist government. The South Sudanese refugee leaders and Ethiopian officials met in Gambella for three days and discussed the overall political agenda of the SPLM/A rebels and the issues of the refugees.[7] Among the South Sudanese refugee leaders were Dr. Colonel John Garang, Akwot Atem, Samuel Gai Tut, Captain Salva Kiir, Willian Chul Deng, and Bol Kur. The Ethiopian high officials first accused the South Sudanese refugees of terrorizing Ethiopian civilians and committing atrocities. In the memo of the ministry of defense it is stated:

> Your refugees in Ethiopia were not properly registered in accordance with the UN regulations, they violate Ethiopian law, they plunder [the local people], they interfere in [the local] administration. What is your opinion about this? [Answer] We have already heard the plundering and illegal activities of the refugees, and we are disappointed. A man would not have destroyed his own house. We consider these people as destroyers of their own houses. All these deeds are the outcome of lack of awareness. We will correct . . . The Ethiopian problem is our problem. Soon we will separate the fighting forces from the aid receiving refugees. Give us directives and we will implement them. . .[8]

The SPLM/A did not deny the accusation because that was what they were doing. To this very day, the South Sudanese refugees are still involved in the local administration and plundering the local people as they wish. The leaders of SPLM/A made an agreement with Mengistu Haile Mariam, and he provided them with military bases for training, weapons, radios, and different military logistics. The Derg regime also had women, children, and elders registered in different refugee camps in Gambella where they were supported and assisted by the UN agencies.

During this period, the Derg government put hundreds of thousands of refugees, mostly Nuers and Dinkas, in different camps in Gambella, including in Itang, Belpam, and Rukedy camps. The refugees in Itang were

---

7. Bayissa, "Derg-SPLM/A Cooperation," 21
8. Bayissa, "Derg-SPLM/A Cooperation," 22

placed in the lands that belonged to Anywaa of Pokedi, Po-nywaa, and Yetiel. The Swedish Red Cross was opened in Itang to serve the refugees who were settled in the area. They also opened a healthcare center in Itang which became the biggest healthcare center in the area. Even people in Gambella town would go to Itang at that time to get good treatment. The foods provided by the UN and the Swedish Red Cross were also used by the SPLM/A rebels. The numbers of Nuer refugees in Itang were small at that time, but they exponentially increased during the TPLF government. Due to bribery by the Nuer refugees, the TPLF government made an unexpected decision by giving the Nuer refugees residing in Itang five *kebeles*. The other nineteen *kebeles* belonged to the Anywaa people. Mr. Oron Ochala said:

> I was one of the people who went to distribute food in these 5 kebeles given to the Nuer by the TPLF government. One of them had only 47 residents. How could 47 people make a kebele? This was because the TPLF government wanted to weaken the Anywaa people.[9]

The problems in Itang accelerated when the Nuer refugees staying there started claiming themselves to be Ethiopians and requested seats to represent themselves in Gambella's regional parliament. In 2000, the Nuer leaders and some Tigrayans sent elders from Itang and asked for the seats. Thus, they were given three seats, which then made them equal with the Anywaa people who also had three seats. When a deadly conflict took place in 2001 between the Anywaa and Nuer in Itang, the Nuer were given more power by making Itang a special district (*woreda*), separating it from the Anywaa zone.

There were also camps in Pinyudo (Pignudo), Dimma, and Bonga. The military and logistical assistance the Derg regime provided to the SPLM/A was to weaken and overthrow the Numeiri regime. The Ethiopian officers and Airborne commandos trained thousands of SPLA guerrilla fighters at different SPLA military camps in western Ethiopia.[10] The Anywaa people were forced to host those refugees in their lands without their permission because of the relationship between Mengistu's government and the SPLM/A. Those refugee camps were also used as bases for the recruitment of more military. Since the refugees were also armed, they had too much power over the Anywaa host community. Thus, Anywaa

---

9. Interview with Oron Ochala (April 26, 2022).
10. Bayissa, "Derg-SPLM/A Cooperation," 29.

people faced cruel treatments, torture, killings, rape, and looting. The Derg government had done nothing to protect civilians from the SPLM/A forces. As Bayissa stated:

> The Derg and the SPLA cooperated with one another and the entire Gambella region was under a kind of their joint administration.[11]

The SPLM/A forces would force the Anywaa men to carry ammunition for them. If they refused to do so, they would threaten them using their weapons. During the harvesting seasons, SPLM/A forces would forcefully reap crops from the Anywaa farms and sometimes destroyed farms purposefully to starve the local farmers.

In September 1989, SPLA forces committed one of the worst atrocities in the Pinyudo area, which is located around the Gilo river. During my interview with of one the residents in Pinyudo at that time, Willie Gilo Lumson, he stated:

> I was in Pinyudo during Ajwieli.[12] I remember at night when everyone was sleeping, they [SPLM/A rebels] would go to the farms by the riverbanks and harvest the corn at night. If the farm has sorghum, they would cut them down and take them.[13]

The Derg government was very aware of the illegal activities inflicted on the Anywaa people by the refugees, yet they failed to protect Anywaa civilians. Not only were they looting and destroying local farms, but they would also take food by force during market days. The incident in Pinyudo took place around 1989 or 1990. During a normal market day, one of the Dinkas went to the Anywaa market and took a biscuit from a young girl who was selling. Without paying the young girl, he opened it and started eating. When the girl asked him for the money, he refused to pay her. She repeatedly asked him to pay her. Then, he dropped the piece of biscuit left in his hand and crushed it with his foot by stepping on it. This angered the Anywaa men who were at the market, and they beat up the Dinka man. He then ran to the camp as fast as he could and told the rest of the armed refugees that he was beaten by a group of Anywaa men. The refugees picked up their arms and marched to the market and started shooting at any Anywaa they saw. Men, women, and children were brutally murdered without any intervention by the Ethiopian government. A very rare case where refugees

11. Bayissa, "Derg-SPLM/A Cooperation," 32.
12. *Ajwieli* is an Anywaa plural word to refer to the Dinkas.
13. Interview with Willie Gilo Lumson (January 18, 2021).

The Refugees in Anywaa Lands

under UNHCR would murder civilians without the government protecting its civilians. According to Prevent Genocide International, over seven hundred Anywaa women and children were massacred by the armed Sudanese refugees. That became one of the deadliest attacks by the Sudanese refugees. Four days later, the SPLA also opened another attack in Itang near the refugee camp, and sixty people were killed. They also killed fourteen people in Akado village and burnt women and children.[14] All these atrocities were committed by the refugees to the Anywaa people without any protection or intervention from the Ethiopian government.

In Baat-Openo, the destruction of refugees caused Anywaa people to leave their lands and migrate to safe areas. During my interview with Oron Ochala (who grew up in Cham) on April 16, 2022, he said:

> In 1987 during the civil war, the Sudanese rebels were defeated by the Arabs, and Jikaw was burned down by the Arabs. Jikaw was one of the Anywaa lands that was used by the Sudanese rebels at that time. The Anywaa people ran, and some relocated to a village called Pinykeew.[15]

From February 7, 1987, SPLA continuously attacked Jikaw and attempted to capture the town for forty-seven days. But the Sudanese forces overwhelmed them and caused them to retreat to Gambella. The Sudanese armies entered Gambella and burned the houses and farms and destroyed the police station in Gambella Jikaw. This led to the relocation of Jikaw woreda to Tuleth, closer to Nyikwo and Aduujwoki. According to Oron, people like Obwodo Cham, Dakiec Okwori, and Aganya Ojulu were sent to Tuleth by the government to work there as government officials. The Derg government put rebels on the border starting from Asosa or Assosa all the way to Gambella borders. When Asosa was invaded and controlled by the EPLF-OLF on January 5, 1990, with the support of the Sudanese army, the SPLA supported the Derg to keep the areas under their control.[16] The camps were put at the borders to help the Derg government create a buffer zone. After the damage that was done to the Anywaa people in Jikaw, they were not able to go back to Jikaw; thus it was renamed "Lare" by the Nuer refugees who settled in it. The Anywaa people only went back to Jikaw after the downfall of the Derg government in 1991. One of the benefits that the Derg regime gained by supporting the SPLM/A movement was the buffer area

14. Bayissa, "Derg-SPLM/A Cooperation," 33.
15. Interview with Oron Ochala (April 26, 2022).
16. Bayissa, "Derg-SPLM/A Cooperation," 39.

that SPLM/A created by fighting the OLA (the Oromo Liberation Army) and GPLM (Gambella People's Liberation Movement). These two groups were fighting the Derg regime and launching guerilla wars from the Upper Nile and Blue Nile. I will discuss more about the GPLM in chapter seven.

The OLA was established in 1973 by the Oromo nationalists with the mission to struggle against what they refer to as "the Abyssinian colonial rule."[17] In the early 1880s, Menelik had conquered many territories in the south and west and imposed his rules on the Oromo people. Historically, the Oromo people had been following the *gada* system. This was influenced by King Menelik II during his quest to expand the Ethiopian state. The Oromo land became a "mengist" state, and they were forced to pay taxes and supply their landlords with butter, oxen, ram, and the best grains.[18] This led to a lot of resentment by the Oromo people toward Menelik and the Abyssinian Empire. Thus, the OLF organization was established to fight the Derg regime, which was contradictory to their mission since Mengistu Haile Mariam was an Oromo himself. The government of Sudan supported the OLA and GPLM as they fought the guerilla wars against Mengistu Haile Mariam in the 1980s. As a return and payback for the government of Sudan, the OLA and GPLM fought the SPLA forces in the Gambella area. This caused the SPLA to take even more revenge and commit atrocities on the Anywaa civilians living in Gambella. To this day, SPLA's atrocities toward the Anywaa people have never been addressed, and nobody was held accountable. The Derg government allowed these cruel treatments of the Anywaa people, and he also labeled the Anywaa *wenbede*, which means "bandits."

The first Nuer refugee who was sponsored by the UN to come to Gambella and attended Gambella High School was called Mr. Tumoro. He was in a new refugee camp at the back of Rasgobana School by the UNHCR. This new refugee camp was then given a name: "Newland." This was to emphasize that this was a new land for the settlement of refugees Nuer students. But the area is originally known by the local indigenous as Cangkwaar and Ye-cwaay or Ichuai. Mark Cuol was also one of the very first Nuer to arrive in Gambella town. He lived in Cangkwaar as well, closer to where the current Gambella University is located. According to the former president of Gambella Okello Akway, there were very few Nuer who arrived in Gambella

---

17. "Mission."
18. Bayissa, "Derg-SPLM/A Cooperation," 36.

town and were not sponsored by the UN.[19] He attended high school together with them, and some of them even lived in Gog woreda with the Anywaa people. Among those who arrived in Gambella town without the sponsorship of the refugee program were Bol Get, Bol Lual, Niel Gach, and Chuol Tut. But people like Dr. Kong and Mr. Timothy were sponsored by the UN under the refugee program. Dr. Kong studied his medical doctorate through the sponsorship of the UN at that time. All the refugee students who were sponsored by the UNHCR lived in Cangkwaar by the UNHCR compound, and that's how Newland came to exist. When GPLM and TPLF took control of Gambella in 1991, all Nuer in Cangkwaar left and moved back to the SPLA liberated area in Sudan. Two years later, they came back to Gambella town in larger numbers and settled in Cangkwaar again. Due to consistent conflicts and rock-throwing between the Anywaa and Nuer in the area, the Anywaa people were forced to leave Cangkwaar and Ye-cwaay (*Ichuai*) area. As the number of Nuer refugees increased in Cangkwaar, the demographics of Gambella started to change significantly.

---

19. Mr. Okello Akway was the president of Gambella from 2003 to 2004.

Chapter 7

The Birth of the GPLM Party

THE ETHIO-SOMALI WAR TOOK place in 1977, when Somalia waged war to take Ogaden from Ethiopia. The Somali National Forces crossed into Ethiopia and carried out attacks in Degahbour, Kebridehar, Warder, and Godey, and they took control of Jijiga and a large part of the western region.[1] During my interview with Oron Ochala, he stated:

> The Anywaa people will always remember this war as the war that finished many Anywaa. This was the war that some people who survived had their fingernails left behind. At that time, when Derg militaries came, they would go to local *kwaari* (chiefs) (reduced to *balabat*) and ask for specific numbers of men they wanted, and the *kwaari* had no choice but to give them the numbers that they were looking for.[2]

After training the Anywaa men, they would send them to the frontline as quickly as possible. Compared to the highlander Ethiopians, the Anywaa men are very tall and bigger in size. Thus, most of them were used by their leaders to carry heavy weapons, and mostly fought in the front lines where the toughest fighting was. Oron Ochala continued and said:

> Another reason that led to the loss of many Anywaa men was that they were very hard to blend within the communities in the western region. So, they had to fight to the end because they had nowhere to go. When the fight got harder, other light-skinned

---

1. Muhumad and Siraj, "Somali Region in Ethiopia," 69.
2. Interview with Oron Ochala (April 26, 2022).

The Birth of the GPLM Party

Ethiopians could run and hide among civilians. However, the Anywaa would fight to death because they had darker skin, and they were more recognizable by the enemy.[3]

Almost all the Anywaa men who were sent to fight in the Ethio-Somali war never returned to Gambella.

When the northern war intensified in the early 1980s, the Derg regime was forced to recruit more army members to face the EPLF. In 1985, the EPLF took an offensive and expelled the Ethiopian forces from the very strategic town of Barentu.[4] This was when Mengistu Haile Mariam was forced to gather everything, and all the force he had, to take back Barentu and Tessenei. They called this *olum neger wede thor ginbar*, meaning, "all and everything to the war front." During the military recruitment, the young Anywaa men and women were forcefully recruited from their villages, even if they were the main provider and the ones taking care of the farming, fishing, and hunting for the families. The men—and even women—were taken from their homes for mandatory service in the military bands. The women had to leave their children behind, and they were sent to the fronts. The casualties were very high among the Anywaa men since they were used as shields in the front lines. Hence those who survived returned home crippled and unable to farm. Those who refused to join the army were imprisoned for at least two years. This made living in Gambella hard for Anywaa young men, forcing many to flee to Sudan. Furthermore, Anywaa men were forced to drop out of schools since the recruitments were held at the secondary schools in Gambella. Cultural Survival reported that in 1985, during a normal day of school, the army officers would get into a classroom in Gambella and forcefully register the names of biggest and strongest Anywaa boys and take them to hospital for checkups.[5] The Anywaa people were mainly targeted for conscription because they were perceived by the government officials as "more Ethiopian" compared to the Nuer.[6] The Nuer avoided this recruitment mainly because of their refugee status in Gambella.

Throughout the recruitment, Anywaa officials were accompanied by the Derg regime military leaders to carry out the recruitment process. Among them was a military leader called Ogut Ajak, *shambel* Pinykeew,

3. Interview with Oron Ochala (April 26, 2022).
4. Cliffe and Davidson, *Long Struggle of Eritrea*, 110.
5. "Anuak Displacement and Ethiopian Resettlement."
6. Feyissa, *Playing Different Games*, 139.

shambel Kwot, *shambel* Akumbuk, and *shambel* Kiru. They would go from school to school looking for young men—stopped buses at the checkpoints and bus stations—and forcefully captured young men and sent them to the war front. Before the day of forced recruitment in Abwobo woreda, Omod Aciir who was one of the officials would warn young people by saying, "If you're bullet resistant, I will meet you tomorrow." He would do this to give out the warning that there would be a recruitment tomorrow, so make sure to leave town. Omod Aciir had saved so many youths' lives from Abwobo woreda using this tactic. As the fighting intensified, many recruits from Gambella were sent to Eritrea, and they were finished there; many people did not return to Gambella. Some young people who refused to fight in the war fled to the neighboring country, Sudan. They went to the refugee camp, and many of them joined the Gambella People's Liberation Movement (GPLM) and fought the Derg regime. On the other hand, Nuer people avoided recruitment and did not get involved in the war because they were considered refugees. Opal and Thuwat Pal were Nuer appointed by the Derg government over the Anywaa people to rule Gambella. Opal Lual (Joshua Delual) and Thuwat Pal were appointed to strengthen the relationship that Derg had with the Sudanese refugees and SPLA forces located in Gambella. They were also used as a tool to weaken the Anywaa people and interrogate the Anywaa youths who were also labeled *"wenbede"* and those who were collaborating with GPLM. So, Opal and Thuwat used their administrative position to protect the Nuer youths from the recruitment by labeling them all as refugees.

The Birth of GPLM Party

The Gambella People's Liberation Movement (GPLM) was created by the Anywaa elites in 1979 during the Derg regime. GPLM was created to fight the Derg regime for various reasons such as the forced military recruitment of the Anywaa people, giving Nuer power to rule in Gambella, SPLA and refugee atrocities against the Anywaa civilians in Gambella, the destruction of the Anywaa people royalty and traditions, and the cruel treatment by the Derg forces against the Anywaa people. When settlers came to Gambella in 1984 without the knowledge of Gambella people, it became one of the reasons that GPLM became very active. During my interview with Commander Bare Agid on August 30, 2022, he said:

The Birth of the GPLM Party

> On 18 August 1971, before fourth grade, Derg militias were brought from Itang to Pokumo, and they were so abusive toward the students. They sometimes opened fire at the students, and we would run away as they chased after us. When you get caught, they would beat you and force you to pay for the bullets that were fired.[7]

Bare Agid started to feel strongly about his people because of the ways that they were treated by the Derg militias. According to him, he was not happy about what the Derg militias were doing to the students and civilians, so he decided to run to Sudan along with a group of people. Bare Agid and the group that he traveled with were questioned by the government of Sudan as to why they were there. Bare stated that they told the government of Sudan about the cruel treatment of the Anywaa people by the Derg and SPLA rebels. Thus, the government of Sudan allowed them to stay in Sudan, and they were put in a new refugee camp in Melekal.

In the month of February in 1980, Bare Agid, Owar Geydo, Obongo Onak, Deng Obongo, Okok Okello, and Didumo Obang went to Cham village and got three weapons. One weapon belonged to Bare Agid, one to his uncle, Wang Ocang, and the other one to Owar Geydo. After getting three weapons, they went to the other villages: Pinykeew, Edeni, Pinyngiew, Pojoo, Emidho, Pinymoo, Ilea, and Ponywaa and tried to talk and recruit people from these areas. Bare Agid stated:

> One of our goals was to connect with the Anywaa people who were in the local militia and convince them to help us with this movement that we were starting.[8]

However, the local Anywaa militias were not willing to help them. When they got to Ponywaa, they were rejected by the Ponywaa people. This group of six opened the very first attack on Derg militias in Birhaneselam military camp. According to Oron Ochala, this group of six were overwhelmed by the Derg militia, and they were forced to retreat. On the same night, Bare Agid and his group went to Cham village. When they arrived at the gate of Cham village, everyone was sleeping including the militias. Oron Ochala said:

> It was very unusual that everyone was sleeping at that time. It made me believe that they were using kunyjuur.[9]

---

7. Interview with Commander Bare Agid (August 30, 2022).
8. Interview with Commander Bare Agid (August 30, 2022).
9. *Kunyjuur (Kugnjuur)* is a magic which the Anywaa believed can prevent you from

Barï Agid and the other five people entered through the gate and went to the Kebele where they opened fire at the highlander teachers and killed them. According to Bare Agid, his brother Kwot Agid was still in Malakal Camp during the attack in Birhaneselam and Cham village. Bare Agid said:

> We came back to Gambella because we didn't want the Derg militias on Anywaa land. They were also committing atrocities on the local young people, killing, and opening fire at them for no reason. We didn't want *adïma*.[10]

The Gambella People's Liberation Movement (GPLM) was created to resist the oppression of the Derg regime. According to Bare Agid, they wanted the Derg militias to leave the Anywaa land so that the Anywaa people could get back to their normal way of life where they were ruled by chiefs and kings. After the attack in Cham village, Bare Agid and his team went back to Sudan.

In 1981, GPLM attacked the village of Edeni, and took some villagers with them to the Sobat (the Anywaa called the place *Nyirwaadha*). At that time, this area was under the control of the Sudanese military (the Arabs). Oron Ojulu said:

> When the GPLM took people from Edeni, there was one Nuer among the people. The Nuer was forced to carry things for them, and they didn't kill him.[11]

Three months later, the Nuer escaped to Ethiopia and told the Derg militias that the Anywaa *wenbedes* were in *Nyirwaadha*. The Nuer man led them and showed where the GPLM forces were located. The Derg militias ambushed the GPLM forces and destroyed the camps. That was the very first sudden attack by the Derg militias which left David Oliimi, the leader of GPLM, dead. The GPLM forces were scattered, and all the documents in David Oliimi's tent were taken by the Derg militias and sent to Addis Ababa. In February of 1982, the Derg militias destroyed Olaaw village, and another important member of GPLM named Baadha was killed, and his head was cut off and displayed to the Anywaa civilians in Gog district. This

---

getting hit by a bullet during the fight, and makes your enemies go to sleep when you are present. The Anywaa also believe that *Kunyjuur* can use nature such as strong wind or rains against the enemy (Interview with Oron Ochala [April 26, 2022]).

10. *Adima* is an Anywaa word for oppression (Interview with Commander Bare Agid [August 30, 2022]).

11. Interview with Oron Ochala (April 26, 2022).

The Birth of the GPLM Party

was to warn the civilians about what the government can do to anyone who joins the rebels. After this, many Anywaa people from Jor, Gog, Cham, Pinykeew, Nyikwo, and many other Anywaa villages emigrated to Sudan to flee from the Derg regime and stayed in the refugee camp in Malakal. According to Oron Ochala, all the GPLM members also moved back to the camp, including people like Oguta Adiw and Ojulu Gaala. GPLM stayed inactive until they met the Oromo Liberation Front (OLF). Bare Agid said:

> We met the OLF group in late 1982. We had a good relationship in the beginning with them. They helped us with ammunition and food, and we all shared information.[12]

This alliance between the GPLM and OLF was created based on a common interest, which was to fight the Derg government. The goal of the OLF group was to fight against what they called "Amhara imperialism," while the GPLM were fighting to get the *gaala*[13] out of their land and stop the Derg's and refugees' atrocities on the Anywaa. Though they were both fighting the Derg government, these two groups had very different goals, and their relationship did not last very long. Bare Agid said:

> The relationship ended when the OLF group said that the Anywaa people should be black Oromo.[14]

The GPLM took this suggestion as another *adïma* (oppression) that the Oromo people wanted to impose on the Anywaa people. Thus, the two groups separated bitterly from each other. In 1984, the Tigray People's Liberation Front (TPLF) created an alliance with the GPLM based on the mutual agreement that after the downfall of the Derg regime, all regions would independently decide for themselves and rule themselves. According to Bare Agid, they were happy with the idea because that's what they wanted for the Anywaa people: to independently govern themselves.

According to Oron Ochala, over eighty members of GPLM were trained after the agreement, and they were released in 1986. Among the people who were trained in the first round were Otongi Kaga, Omod Ojulu, and Okello Oman. GPLM became very active again in the Gambella area after the alliance with the TPLF group. Mr. Oron Ochala said:

---

12. Interview with Commander Bare Agid (August 30, 2022).

13. *Gaala* is a general word that the Anywaa people use to call the highlanders, light-skinned Ethiopians, which put Oromo people under the same categories.

14. Interview with Commander Bare Agid (August 30, 2022).

> Whenever they came at night we would know because the night would be too unusually quiet, and even dogs would cease barking at night. Some people believed that the GPLM were using kunyjuur to put people to sleep whenever they came to the village.[15]

Police post in Itang woreda was attacked by the GPLM in 1986, and highlander state employees were killed in the attack. In 1987, Okello Oman and Ojulu Ogaala spied in Gambella town, and GPLM carried out a well-organized attack in the Kumthalebash military camp located in Abol town. The GPLM burned down the camp and targeted the Kambatha settlers in the Abol area which led to many civilian deaths. After the attack, the GPLM headed to the village of Pinykeew and forcefully took young people with them as they returned to their base in Sudan.

The attack on the Kumthalebash military camp and the killing of Kambatha settlers angered the Derg government, and they started suspecting the Anywaa officials in the government and civilians in the town. Among the suspected people were Agwa Alemu, Ojulu Obang, Ogal Oman, Nyigwo Wajoi, Ajaangween, Okello Oman, Okongo Ochan, Odol Lwal, and Jima Ojulu and his wife Akwata Omod. Kwot Wagole was killed by Thuwat Pal, and about thirty suspected Anywaa people were captured that day. The Derg government went on and killed Anywaa young men around Openo Bridge on the same day, and they were labeled as *wenbede* (meaning "outlaws"). According to Markakis, eighty Anywaa executed in Gambella town, followed by a wave of political repression.[16] Agwa Alemu and other prisoners were interrogated and tortured by the Derg militias in the prison. Agwa Alemu was forced to walk on nails with his bare feet, and severely beaten. The following day, the Derg officials met and planned to transfer Agwa Alemu to Metu Prison, which was called *Alem Bekagn* at that time, meaning, "I am done with the world!" During that night, a Tigrayan security guard helped Agwa Alemu escape, and they both left the town at night. Agwa Alemu stayed hidden in the Golli area since he was not able to walk for long distances due to his swollen feet. Willie Gilo Lumson said:

> When everyone in town heard that Agwa Alemu was not in the prison, the town went too quiet that morning.[17]

---

15. Interview with Oron Ochala (April 26, 2022).
16. Markakis, *Ethiopia*, 224.
17. Interview with Willie Gilo Lumson (January 18, 2021).

The Birth of the GPLM Party

To let his family know that he was alive, Agwa Alemu sent a letter to his friend through a farmer that he was staying with, and the letter was given to his friend Pastor Olul Owiti. In the letter, he wanted Pastor Olul to let Pastor Akway Ochudho know that he is not dead, and he also wanted some painkiller medicine for his feet. After his feet got better, Agwa Alemu escaped to Sudan and joined the GPLM camp. The other thirty Anywaa prisoners, including one woman with a newborn baby, were taken to Metu Prison and then relocated to Jimma Prison. In early 1990, Ajaangween became sick and died in Jimma Prison.

Agwa Alemu, who became the leader of the GPLM, went to Malakal and created an alliance with the Ethiopian People's Revolutionary Democratic Front (EPRDF). GPLM forces were then sent to Mekele for training. Bare Agid said:

> After our training was done in Mekele, we came in through Nekemte and came to Bonga. The other team came in from Abush and took on Gambella.[18]

The fighting got harder from all fronts against the Derg government. On May 21, 1991, Mengistu Haile Mariam was advised by the United States to leave the country to prevent more deaths. Oron Ochala said:

> During that day, we were all listening to Mengistu Haile Mariam on the national radio. He talked for hours and hours before he left the country.[19]

The GPLM and EPRDF fighters from Abush entered Gambella and took control of the town. The SPLA armies who were still in Gambella fought back, but they eventually were defeated and retreated to their liberated areas in Sudan (part of today's South Sudan). Thuwat Pal escaped to Sudan on May 27, 1991, leaving Opal Lual in Gambella. All the Nuer in the Cangkwaar area escaped to the Sudan border, which was under the control of SPLA at that time. The GPLM and EPRDF forces took control of all of Gambella, and the communist Derg was overthrown. These two forces stayed in two different places: the GPLM forces located at the former Sudanese consulate compound in the center of Gambella town, while the EPRDF forces stayed in a new camp around Tiet-baale area.

When the Nuer escaped to the SPLA occupied areas in Sudan, there were few Nuer left in the Cangkwaar area. Among them was Biel Keyliic

---

18. Interview with Commander Bare Agid (August 30, 2022).
19. Interview with Oron Ochala (April 26, 2022).

who was married to an Anywaa woman named Ajulu Nyonak, and Deng Dung who was a member of Mekane Yesus church. The generals of GPLM forces brought those Nuer who stayed in Gambella and tried to escort them to the GPLM base (where Grand-Hotel is currently located). When Nuer understood that they were heading to the GPLM base, they stopped walking. Then, the GPLM generals opened fire at them and killed them all. An eyewitness, Willie Gilo Lumson, stated:

> They came with multiple Nuer in front of them. But, when they got closer to the former Sudanese consulate in Gambella town, the Nuer refused to walk, fearing that they would be killed if they went to the GPLM base. It didn't take very long; I was watching when they opened fire and killed them, while the TPLF forces were also watching. I would say that what they did showed a lack of discipline.[20]

This incident was immediately reported to the federal government in Addis Ababa, and Meles Zenawi ordered the regional president Agwa Alemo to hand those GPLM generals to the EPRDF forces in Gambella to be taken to Addis Ababa. President Agwa Alemu didn't hand in the generals to the federal government, stating that the country was still in the midst of transition and chaos, and mistakes do happen. The federal government also didn't have a federal prison at that time, and the country was still in an unstable situation.

Another incident occurred in Gambella on the night of August 20, 1992. There was a member of GPLM named Obang Andaare who was off-duty that night. Obang Andaare had an argument about a cow with a TPLF soldier around the Tier-Kidi neighborhood, and he was shot and killed by the TPLF soldier. When the GPLM forces heard about that, they immediately armed themselves and opened an attack on the TPLF forces in Gambella. Dr. Magn Cham said:

> I, myself, am a living witness for what took place that night. I was in a local bar in the city that night enjoying my hot tea when I heard the first shot. And after that a good two to three hours gun fight erupted between GPLM fighters and TPLF fighters. The city was turned upside down by the sounds of artillery and rocket propelled grenades (RPGs). When it was all over, one GPLM fighter and twelve TPLF fighters laid dead, and the death toll on

---

20. Interview with Willie Gilo Lumson (January 18, 2021).

the civilians who got caught in the crossfire was even greater (SudanTribune, 2006).[21]

The GPLM fighters went on and killed the highlanders who were selling goods in Owalinga (today called "market center") as revenge. The death toll was so high that they ran out coffins and burial materials. That was the response of GPLM forces: revenge for a GPLM member Obang, who was killed by the TPLF soldier. When the federal government received the information, Meles Zenawi asked the regional president, Agwa Alemu, to immediately hand in the GPLM fighters who were responsible for the killing of civilians. Since this was a military incident, Agwa Alemu responded by holding the GPLM generals who were on duty that day accountable. Instead of sending those generals to the federal prison, Agwa Alemu put them in Gambella prison. The GPLM leaders who were put in jail were Omod Tutker, Kwot Agid, Otongi Kaaga, Omod Ojulukway, and a few others. From that day on, the relationship between the GPLM and TPLF (EPRDF) started to sour and got worse. The EPRDF, which started practicing Tigrayan hegemony, wanted to fully enforce its ruling over regions like Gambella. But the GPLM, which also had hegemonic aspirations, made it harder for the TPLF to freely impose their rules on Gambella. Thus, the GPLM put them under the category of *gaale*, whom they fought to leave Gambella and allow Gambella people to independently rule themselves.

When GPLM won the first election of 1992, Anywaa people dominated the politics of Gambella, and they led the region with their own GPLM forces. The EPRDF was not happy with this, even though it was what they agreed on with the GPLM—that every region would have the right to independently rule themselves. Dr. Magn Cham stated that both the TPLF and highlanders did not trust the Anywaa-led government and its military wing. One of the examples that Dr. Magn Cham said was when a highlander is denied a job by an Anywaa manager, they would go to the TPLF with their complaints instead of going to the regional labor department office. This led to mistrust between the federal government and the GPLM leadership. In the same year of 1992, the Nuer SPLA continued fighting with the GPLM forces in Itang district. When the GPLM forces were short on ammunition, they went to the *therfi shi-aleka* (the EPRDF compound in Gambella town). But the TPLF general refused to send ammunition to the GPLM forces stating that there was no ammunition in the storage. On that same day, a GPLM member named Wiith saw a military truck parked by the

21. Sudan Tribune (August 3, 2006)

Total gas station in Gambella, and the driver was a TPLF soldier in his uniform. With curiosity, Wiith asked what the driver was carrying, to which he honestly stated that he was carrying weapons and ammunition that needed to be taken to Mekele. As a GPLM member, Wiith was confused why their forces were having a shortage of ammunition while the TPLF forces were looting the weapons and ammunition in Gambella. This was the time when TPLF was looting machines, weapons, ammunition, and any technology from each region and taking them to Tigray. Wiith called the GPLM compound and told them about the ammunition and weapons that were about to be taken to Mekele. The GPLM general then increased the number of forces at the Openo Bridge checkpoint, which was the only exit to the road to Metho. When the driver of the truck approached the checkpoint, he was told to turn the truck around and park it at the GPLM base (the former Sudanese consulate). Without any argument, the TPLF soldier turned the car around and parked it by the GPLM base. When the federal government heard about this, they sent a higher number of TPLF soldiers to Gambella town, and the fighting erupted between the two forces, leading to higher casualties on both sides. The GPLM compound was taken over by the TPLF forces, and the GPLM forces were relocated to Wibur, next to Gamkidi. As the GPLM forces prepared to attack again and get back to their compound, the Anywaa elders from church and community such as Pastor Olul Owiti, Oriet Agure or Hailemariam Teklemariam, and Nunu Ogud Nyigwo talked to the GPLM forces and convinced them not to fight the TPLF forces in the town. This was when the Abol camp was opened, and all the GPLM forces were relocated there.

The Birth of the GPLM Party

This picture was taken in Gambella town on August 30, 2022. Jekap Omod on the left, Commander Bare Agid in the middle, and Omod Ochan Oboya on the right. Commander Bare Agid was born in a village called Cham in Baat-Openo. His mother's name is Agala Okok, and she was from a village called Pinykok. His father, Agid Ojwato, was from one of the Pinykeew's villages called Pinyjoo. He attended school at Birhaneselam during Haile Selassie and attended school in Pokumo at the missionaries' school of Akado. Bare Agid was one of the first people who started the GPLM organization and fought against the Derg government. He was also one of the Anywaa heroes who fought in multiple wars against the TPLF government after the Anywaa genocide, the Murle, Nuer invaders, and the OLF. Ochan Oboya is a member of the GPLM and an Anywaa hero as well.

Chapter 8

The Downfall of the GPLM Party

AGWA ALEMU WAS AN Anywaa politician who played a very crucial role in the history of the Anywaa leadership post-Anywaa monarchy era. He received his political education in Cuba and became a member of the Marxist Waz League. When Agwa Alemu finished his education in Cuba, he returned to Ethiopia, and he was appointed as the administrator of Jikaw district by the Derg government. When the relationship between the Marxist Waz League and the Derg government went sour, Agwa Alemu was kicked out from his position and sent to jail. After he was released from jail, Agwa Alemu worked for the UNHCR and then was reappointed to his previous position as the administrator of Jikaw district.

During the attack in Itang and Abol in 1986 and 1987 respectively, Agwa Alemu was suspected by the Derg government of collaborating with the GPLM organization, and he was put in prison. Agwa Alemu joined the GPLM after he escaped from the prison and became the leader of GPLM. When the GPLM and EPRDF forces took over Gambella after the fall of the Derg regime, Agwa Alemu was appointed the president of Gambella during the transition period. During this period, the different forces in Ethiopia didn't have a stable budget from the federal government; thus, each region was responsible for the necessities of their local forces including food and monthly salaries. When GPLM forces were relocated to the new camp in Abol woreda, the local government didn't have enough food and necessities for the soldiers. Oron Ochala said:

The Downfall of the GPLM Party

The only food available for the GPLM forces was ground wheat flour and berbere spice [an Ethiopian spice made with chili peppers and other ingredients]. The GPLM forces would cook the wheat flour and eat it with berbere spice mixed with water.[1]

Some GPLM forces started hunting and farming to get food and earn money. The local business owners, and civilians were supposed to be the source of income for the local forces since they didn't have a stable budget yet during the transition period. But the business owners, who were mostly highlanders, were not supportive of the GPLM forces, and they didn't support them.

According to Bare Agid, the GPLM forces tried three times to meet with their president, Agwa Alemu, to address the issue of the lack of food, but President Agwa Alemu was not willing to meet with them. Bare Agid said:

> Having meetings is very important. We never had any meeting with President Agwa Alemu since we took over Gambella. Agwa Alemu was not willing to meet with his soldiers, which created many problems between the forces and the president.[2]

President Agwa Alemu went to Addis Ababa for a meeting to discuss all the incidents that occurred in Gambella. After he came back, the relationship between him and his GPLM forces got even worse. The GPLM forces complained that Agwa Alemu was enjoying all the money and living comfortably, while they were left alone in the camp to starve. On July 11, 1992, about 360 GPLM soldiers went to Gambella town fully armed with the intention to take Oguta Adiw, Ojulu Akwor, Onugi, Odol Lwaal, and Agwa Alemu to the camp. When they arrived in Gambella town, they captured the leaders that they were looking for except President Agwa Alemu. The elders such as pastor Olul Owiti and Ariet Ojulu (Bipang) went to them and asked them about what they wanted. According to Willie Gilo Lumson, when the GPLM forces stated that they came because they were not provided with food, the business owners in the city contributed all they could and gave it to them. Most of them took the food items (cows, sheep, and a few bags of wheat) and returned to the camp.

However, at about 8 p.m., one group of GPLM forces went to Agwa Alemu home where he was staying with his family. When they entered

---

1. Interview with Oron Ochala (April 26, 2022).
2. Interview with Commander Bare Agid (August 30, 2022).

Agwa's home, they exchanged fire, leaving Agwa Alemu and one person from the GPLM group dead. The bodyguard of Agwa Alemu, who was from the Majang tribe, was also killed. After killing their own president, the same GPLM group went to the prison and released their leaders who were put in jail during the conflict that led to the death of many highlanders. Among the GPLM leaders who were released include Kwot Agid, Omod Tutker, Otongi Kaaga, and Omod Ojulukway. Bare Agid said:

> The death of Agwa Alemu was unnecessary, and he should have never died. Agwa was killed by the people who were telling him not to meet with his soldiers.[3]

Even though there was no individual who was officially held accountable for the killing of Agwa Alemu, Mr. Okok Ojulu was accused by the relatives and the daughter of Agwa Alemu such as Mr. Kiru Abella and Beerjack Alemu. They claimed that Mr. Okok Ojulu was responsible for the death of President Agwa Alemu. However, Mr. Okok Ojulu strongly condemned and denied the accusations made by the individuals who accused him of killing Agwa Alemu.

The Battle of Abol

After the death of Agwa Alemu, the federal government was informed about it, and they sent officials to Gambella by helicopter to confirm the death of the president. Two days later, a group of *Agazi* commandos from Jimma were sent to Gambella town. They headed to Abol GPLM camp in the early morning without anybody noticing them. Bare Agid said:

> Under my command, I had 120 soldiers, and we were in a place called Aguuri. When juure arrived at the camp, Ajak and Kwot Agid were staying on the farm located at the modern day of Abol town. Kwot Agid came to me and told me that *juure*[4] were at the camp.[5]

The first bullet was shot around 3 a.m. and hit the commander Omod Tutker in the head, and non-stop firings followed from both sides. According to Oron Ochala, they could even hear gunshots from a very long distance.

3. Interview with Commander Bare Agid (August 30, 2022).

4. *Juure* is the Dha-Anywaa plural for *jur* which means a "foreigner." The Anywaa people refer to non-Anywaa as foreigners since they consider them to be outsiders.

5. Interview with Commander Bare Agid (August 30, 2022).

The Downfall of the GPLM Party

Nyingiew and Otongi Kaaga were among the people who were shot and killed at this battle. The fighting lasted for the whole day. Commander Bare Agid said:

> This was one of the toughest fights we fought, and we lost eighty people, but the number of commandos they lost from their side could not be counted. They lost so many soldiers in that war, and they still hold grudges about that to this day.[6]

At that point, the GPLM fighters were out of ammunition already, and they were using their enemy's weapons. As the fighting got tougher, the GPLM forces retreated to a village called Pomooli. About eleven of their wounded fighters were captured by the *Agazi* commandos.[7] Bare Agid was hit by four bullets in that war alone, and they went all the way to Pochala, South Sudan.

At that time, King Agada was ruling Adongo Kingdom. He allowed the GPLM forces to stay in Adongo and gave them asylum. The Anywaa elders in South Sudan such as Paul Anade[8] negotiated with the Meles Zenawi, and they reached an agreement to bring the GPLM forces back to Gambella. People like Peter Aman and other GPLM members were brought back to Ethiopia and stationed in their previous camp in Abol. Based on the agreement that they had, they were provided bed sheets and paid two hundred *birrs* monthly. The GPLM forces were then integrated into the national army in the year of 1992 and deployed to different parts of Ethiopia. This became the end of the GPLM forces' presence in Gambella and the beginning of the GPLM Party destruction by the federal government. Only one GPLM member returned to Gambella, but most of them fought in the wars of Ogaden and Badme. Most of them died during the Ogaden war in 1994. Mr. Oron Ochala said:

---

6. Interview with Commander Bare Agid (August 30, 2022).

7. *Agazi* commandos are named after one of the TPLF Agazi (Zeru) Gessesse. These forces were only sent to the front when there was a big threat against the TPLF regime. They are loyal to the regime and well-trained to encounter any threat. They also played a big role in countering terrorism in Somalia.

8. Paul Anade was one of the Anywaa politicians who created the Gambella Liberation Front (GLF) in 1976. This political organization included Anywaa elites such as Philip Odiel, Simon Mori, Philip Akiyu, and Agud Obang. Paul Anade was a MP in the South Sudanese government; Philip Odiel was the governor of the Upper Nile region; Simon Mori was a minister in the Southern Sudanese government; Agud Obang was a general in the Sudanese army; and Philip Akiyu was an administrator of Pochala district (Feyissa, *Playing Different Games*, 42–43).

Great fighters like Ojulu Oboli died during the Ogaden war. He was a very clever person when it comes to education as well. Other people like Oman Ochan and Oman Owaa died during the war of Badme; they were burned from a distance because they were operating on heavy weapons.[9]

Among the few members of GPLM who joined the national army later and fought the war of Badme include Bare Agid and Bach Odier.

The Downfall of GPLM

In 1992, the Anywaa people had a political dominance in Gambella after their organization, GPLM, fought and took over Gambella after the fall of Derg regime. Out of twenty regional ministers there were fifteen Anywaa, three Nuer, one Majang and one Komo.[10] The prime minister of Ethiopia, Meles Zenawi, saw the GPLM organization and the Anywaa people as a threat to their TPLF political hegemony. After integrating the GPLM forces into the national army, Meles Zenawi had to also diminish the Anywaa political dominance in Gambella. The best way to accomplish this was to use the Nuer elites as a tool to weaken the Anywaa people and destroy the GPLM Party. During the election of 1995, the GPLM won, but the election was rigged in favor of EPRDF. Those who were loyal to the TPLF government were then put to power. Then, the federal government forcefully changed the name GPLM to GPLP (Gambella People's Liberation Party). The goal of the federal government was to get rid of the GPLM Party entirely and install a new regional government that is loyal to the TPLF government. In 1998, Meles Zenawi went further and merged the GPLP with GPDUP (Gambella People's Democratic Unity Party), an organization created by the Nuer to oppose the GPLM in 1992 and formed the GPDF (Gambella People's Democratic Front). This was a success for the Nuer elites because it gave them political recognition, and moreover it heralded EPRDF's enhanced political control over Gambella region.[11] This angered the Anywaa elites, which led to a creation of a new party called Gambella People's Democratic Congress (GPDC).

---

9. Interview with Oron Ochala (April 26, 2022).
10. Dereje, *Experiences of the Gambella*, 220.
11. Zewde, *Society, State, and Identity*, 146.

The Downfall of the GPLM Party

According to Bahru Zewde, the GPDC gained popularity in Anywaa areas, and they became a threat as the second regional election approached.[12] As a result, the EPRDF jailed the prominent leaders of GPDC and rigged the election. On July 7, 2002, a deadly conflict broke out between the Anywaa and Nuer in Itang woreda, when an armed group of Nuer attacked the police station which led to the death of sixty Anywaa. Many Anywaa civilians also lost their lives, since many Nuer were members of SPLA and were fully armed compared to the unarmed Anywaa civilians. The regional government asked the federal government many times to intervene, but the federal government did not respond. The Nuer used this opportunity to ambush and killed as many Anywaa they could in Itang district, since they were unarmed and defenseless. Dozens of Anywaa villages were burned to the ground without any intervention by the federal government. Six months later, the regional president had an "Anywaa elites only" meeting to try to respond to the killing that was taking place. The federal government then accused the Anywaa leaders and elites of inciting and spreading violence among the Anywaa and Nuers in Itang and other mixed settlement areas. So, they responded by jailing all the leaders of Anywaa including the president, Okello Nyigelo.[13] Many Anywaa police were fired because they were accused of participating in the conflicts. This disproportionate imprisonment by the federal government alienated the Anywaa and led to the creation of a rebellion group against the federal government.

The Nuer and Dinka refugees in Pinyudo camp were also involved in the killing of the Anywaa. When women would go out to collect wood for cooking or fetch water, they would get chased by the refugees and sometimes got raped or killed. The Anywaa people of Pinyudo protested and demanded the UNHCR to relocate the refugees into a different camp outside of Pinyudo, but nobody listened to their request. On December 2, 2002, the Anywaa people attacked the camp in Pinyudo, killing about thirty-three refugees. This became a great headache and embarrassment for Ethiopia in front of the international community. The federal government promised the international community to relocate the refugees into a new secure camp and served justice. This led to a mass incarceration of the Anywaa youths, and the federal government started referring to the Anywaa people as *shifta*, which means rebels or bandits. The new site was found in a place

---

12. Zewde, *Society, State, and Identity*, 146.

13. Okello Nyigelo (Gnigelo) was the president of Gambella from August 1997 to 2003. He was a member of the GPDF Party.

called Ogiira. In the early morning of Saturday on December 13, 2003, a vehicle of the Administration for Refugee and Returnee Affairs (ARRA)[14] organization went to check the new site found for the refugees in Ogiira. When they reached a place called Baat-Thiidha by the Abol area, the car was ambushed by unknown gunmen and eight people were killed. Among the dead were seven ARRA officials and an Anywaa driver. This was the incident that led to the Anywaa genocide of December 13, 2003.

14. ARRA is an organization created by the federal government to protect and assist refugees in Ethiopia. It is currently known as the Refugees and Returnees Services (RRS). In Gambella, the RRS has more power than the regional government; they operate the way that they want in the region without the consent of the local indigenous populations. Most Anywaa believe that this organization is carrying out a silent genocide on the Anywaa people using the refugees. They cover up the atrocities that are done to the local Anywaa by the refugees and do nothing to disarm the refugees who keep weapons with them. The December 13, 2003, Anywaa genocide was carried out after ARRA officials were killed by unknown people. The Anywaa people were blamed for their deaths, and they were massacred.

PART 3

Chapter 9

The Anywaa Genocide

AFTER THE DEATH OF seven ARRA officials and an Anywaa driver in a car that was ambushed by unknown gunmen on December 13, 2003, Tadesse HaileSelase from the police department was ordered by the federal forces to go and bring the bodies of the victims to Gambella town. This all happened without the knowledge of the regional president at that time, Okello Akway.[1] The ex-president of Gambella Okello Akway was not informed about the incident. During my interview with Okello Akway, he stated as follows:

> I was never informed by Omod Obang Olom or Tsegaye Beyene. But I felt that something was wrong at that time.[2]

Omod Obang Olom was the head of Gambella police commissioner at that time, and Tsegaye Beyene was a commander from the federal government who oversaw security in Gambella region. The highlanders in Gambella had the information, but the Anywaa people didn't know anything that morning. President Okello Akway was talking to Tsegaye around a place where the current Grand Hotel is located when many Gurage people approached his car and said, "Why don't you start with this one?" That's when things became clearer to the president, but neither Tsegaye Beyene nor the police commissioner told him anything yet. Okello Akway said:

---

1. President Okello Akway was appointed as a temporary president after President Okello Nyigelo was removed from his position. He was a member of the Gambella People's Democratic Congress (GPDC).

2. Interview with Okello Akway (August 29, 2022).

> I heard what the *gurage* people said, but I pretended as if I didn't hear anything because I wanted Tsegaye to tell me himself about what happened.[3]

In order to protect the president of Gambella from what was about to happen, General Tsegaye Beyene took the president to a hotel owned by Abrehet (Mebrahtu), and there were two other generals there already. That was when Tadesse HaileSelase arrived in Gambella town with the bodies of the victims. The dead bodies were on a pickup truck on purpose to make them visible to everyone and fuel anger. Instead of taking the dead bodies to Gambella General Hospital, Tadesse took them to *Mikir Bet* (regional council building) and fired three bullets in the air. Then, Tadesse HaileSelase asked about the president Okello Akway and said:

> Here are the bodies, eat them! Come eat them! If Okello was here, he would have brought these bodies back to life![4]

Okallo Akway was staying with Tsegaye at this time, and there was no information about the people who ambushed the car.

After taking the bodies to *Mikir Bet*, they took them to the police station and then to the general hospital. That was when the killing of the Anywaa people started in the morning by uniformed EPRDF soldiers and some Highlanders. The first Anywaa who was killed was Pastor Okwier Oletho. Pastor Okwier Oletho was one of the most educated Anywaa at that time. During an interview with reporter Agwa Gilo, the wife of pastor Okwier Oletho, Achati Ojulu, stated as follows:

> On Saturday, my husband, Pastor Okwier Oletho, had been in Gambella for a week after he came back from abroad. We were about to visit someone called Okony. That was when Omod Lero called us and informed us that things were not going well in Gambella and that some people were killed. He informed us to maybe stay home and visit later when things get better. My husband told me that we should just go since we were on our way already. When we passed by Okony Nyigwo's house, she told us the same thing that we shouldn't go to Baro-Mado because of the situation. So, I told my husband to go back home, and I went to the hospital to visit Akich's daughter because she was admitted to Gambella general hospital. When I got inside the hospital, I was not able to come back out; two military trucks were brought to the hospital

---

3. Interview with Okello Akway (August 29, 2022).
4. Interview with Okello Akway (August 29, 2022).

The Anywaa Genocide

and blocked everyone from leaving. Then, I saw a team of soldiers in uniforms coming from Buri Market followed by a big number of Highlanders (the capital *H* is to distinguish the Highlanders who were involved in the killing from the other highlander Ethiopians) carrying machetes, knives, axes, and many other things as weapons. They came to Omiininga with Ethiopian soldiers in uniforms, and some headed to my house. I could see them from the hospital, but I was not able to get out. They surrounded my house, and a person who is still living in Gambella today named Adugna poured gas on my house. I was watching them, and my husband was hiding inside with a group of people. They lit up the house and one soldier threw a grenade inside, through the window. The people inside were suffocated with the smoke, and they jumped out of a window. Pastor Okwier Oletho, Cham Obang, Ojulu Omod, and another person called Aciim were captured as I was watching. Most of them were shot and killed by the Ethiopian soldiers as they jumped out and landed on the ground. But they captured my husband and started brutally beating him along the way on the street. By the time they got closer to Akway's house, they continued beating my husband with everything they had in their hands, and he fell. They killed him there, and my heart refused to believe that it was my husband. I could hear them from a distance saying, "*Yet'abatachew*.[5] They claimed this land to be theirs. They will die like dogs today. No one of them should be left alive." That is what I saw with my own eyes and heard.[6]

The killing went on in the Omiininga neighborhood—houses were burned down and smoke filled the sky. Omod Obang and Tsegaye Beyene were staying at Tsegaye's office and keeping the president, Okello Akway, with them. According to Okello Akway, Tsegaye was on the phone the whole time communicating with the commanders who were carrying out the genocide, while Omod Obang was reading him some names from a piece of paper he took out of his pocket. In the afternoon, Okello Akway went to his house to check on his family, and when he got back to Tsegaye's office, Okello Oman[7] was already in the office. He was called to go to Pinyudo with Shambel Amare and carry out the killing in Pinyudo as well. Okello Akway said:

---

5 *Yet'abatachew* is an Amharic insult, similar to saying that "they deserve this s-word."

6. Interview by reporter Agwa Gilo, June 25, 2022.

7. Okello Oman was the president of Gambella from 1992 to 1997, after Agwa Alemu was assassinated.

> When I heard that they were sending a group to Pinyudo to start the killing over there, I asked about what was going on in Pinyudo. They were all busy in the room, and nobody was even paying attention to me. It seems like I didn't exist in the room.[8]

Okello Oman and his team got to Pinyudo, and the first Anywaa person that the federal forces saw was a young man fetching water without knowing anything about what happened in Gambella. They shot him right away and killed him. When the Anywaa police heard about it, they mobilized and started fighting back in Pinyudo. Former president of Gambella, Okello Akway, said:

> At that time, I had no authority anymore, so I just went home to stay with my family. On my way back home, I looked at the street of Dojer Olami, general hospital, Matu mazoria, and the road to Abwobo, and they were all occupied by the Ethiopian federal forces.[9]

This was how the killing started on December 13, 2003. More than 420 Anywaa were killed by the Ethiopian soldiers and Highlanders on this single day, and it was later verified by the Human Rights Watch team that was sent to Gambella town.

The killing and looting continued during the night. On December 14, Okello Akway, with his security, Aballa Odier, went to Omod Obang and Tsegaye Beyene, who were still staying at Tsegaye's office at around 10 a.m. When they arrived at Tsegaye's office, Okello Akway went inside and told them to stop killing. Okello Akway stated as follows:

> I went into the office and told them to stop killing. Then, I asked them why they were killing innocent civilians in Gambella town who had nothing to do with the people who died a few kilometers away from the town in Baat-Thiida. They were shocked and stared at me. Then, Tsegaye said to me that the killers in the forest and those in the town are all the same. So, I asked him if he had proof that those who ambushed the car were from the Anywaa tribe. He never responded or provided any proof to me.[10]

To this day, there is still no evidence which shows that the Anywaa people were responsible for the death of eight ARRA officials. The educated

---

8. Interview with Okello Akway (August 29, 2022).
9. Interview with Okello Akway (August 29, 2022).
10. Interview with Okello Akway (August 29, 2022).

Anywaa men were specifically targeted in response to the death of ARRA officials. Even if Anywaa people were responsible, the only responsible individuals should have been held accountable and brought to justice. As the killing continued, Okello Akway tried to call Almaw Alemeraw, who was at the Federal *Guday* ministry, and also in the Democracy and Security of Federal. Almaw Alemeraw didn't say anything to Okello Akway but referred him to Omod Obang and Tsegaye Beyene, who were carrying out the killing on the ground. Okello Akway said:

> When I didn't get any good response from Almaw Alemeraw, I called Dr. Gebre-Aba Barnabas and told him about the killing that the federal forces were carrying out in Gambella. And I told him that he needed to get those forces out of Gambella.[11]

Dr. Gebre-Aba Barnabas was the Ministry Data of Federal and Civil Security at that time. He responded to Okello Akway thinking that Okello was a part of their plan. Okello Akway stated:

> When Dr. Gebre-Aba Barnabas responded, he thought that I was with them. He said that if things are getting harder, I should call Jimma and bring in more forces. I told him that I was calling him to get the forces in Gambella out and stop killing innocent civilians. I also stated that as a governor of the region, I have no constitutional authority to give orders to the federal forces. Dr. Gebre-Aba Barnabas went so quiet after he heard that. I think he understood that I was not a part of their plan.[12]

On the third day of genocide on December 15, the killing continued, and Omod Obang and Tsegaye were still at their usual place: Tsegaye's office. On the morning of December 15, Shambel Amare, federal forces and the Highlanders were going from house to house hunting the hiding Anywaa men and looting the properties left behind in the Tier-Kidi neighborhood. Shambel Amare stayed at the house of Opiti Cham and used the landline phone to communicate with Tsegaye and Obang. When they found an Anywaa man, they would bring him to Shambel Amare, and he would call Tsegaye and Obang to check if the captured Anywaa's name was on the list. If the name was on the list, they would kill him. Even if the name was not on the list, they would kill him as well, unless they were a member of the EPRDF. The Anywaa men who were the members of the party were taken

---

11. Interview with Okello Akway (August 29, 2022).
12. Interview with Okello Akway (August 29, 2022).

to the Grand Hotel, where they were protected. People like Ojulu Ochala survived because he was a member of the party and was taken to the Grand Hotel. During this day, Okello Akway stated:

> I was going around from my home in Tier-Kidi when I heard a very loud screaming from the house of Ato Okok Ojulu, who was in the federal prison at that time. It was Okok's wife, Nunu, and a person named Dingur crying. There was a group of Oromo people trying to jump over the wall and kill Okok's children. When they saw me, they ran away, and I knocked on the door and told them that it was me. When I got inside, they stopped crying. The children were locked in one room. I told them that they'd be alright, then I went back to my car and went on our way. When we got to the Kulubi area, the Highlander civilians stoned the car that I was in. They were told by Shambel Amare to do so. I asked my driver to slow down the car so I could fire a shot, but he sped up instead. My personal driver, Ngadhe, was jailed already; this was a new highlander driver they gave me.[13]

Aballa Odier and Okello Akway went to Tsegay's office on the third day again, and Okello told both Tsegaye and Omod that he was done with them because it had been three days since they started killing civilians and walked out. They then drove to Mikir Bet, and they were followed by Tsegaye and Omod. When they reached his office in Mikir Bet, Tsegaye followed and walked into his office and said:

> If I am here killing civilians, I want you to write me a letter so I can leave Gambella.[14]

Okello Akway refused to write a letter for him, since he was not the person who invited Tsegaye to Gambella to kill Anywaa people. After Okello Akway refused, Omod Obang said:

> Okello, if you keep talking like this, you will be killed like Agwa Alemu.[15]

This was new information because what was known was that Agwa Alemu was killed by his soldiers for food. But Omod Obang was stating that Okello Akway would be killed like Agwa Alemu. So, the question is, was Agwa Alemu killed by the same TPLF government that carried out the Anywaa genocide?

---

13. Interview with Okello Akway (August 29, 2022).
14. Interview with Okello Akway (August 29, 2022).
15. Interview with Okello Akway (August 29, 2022).

THE ANYWAA GENOCIDE

On December 15, at 8 p.m., Dr. Gebre-Aba Barnabas went on Ethiopian national radio and stated that what was happening in Gambella was a "conflict between the Anywaa and Nuer." The goal of this announcement was to cover up what the Ethiopian government was doing to the Anywaa people, making it a tribal conflict. After one hour of the reporting by Dr. Gebre-Aba Barnabas, an Oromo woman named Asegret Bertha called Okello Akway and informed him about what Dr. Gebre-Aba Barnabas reported through the Ethiopian national radio. "I told her that it was a lie; there was no conflict between Anywaa and Nuer. It was the Ethiopian national forces and some Highlanders killing the Anywaa people," said Okello Akway. Asegret Bertha took Okello Akway to the studio the same night and interviewed him. Okello Akway stated:

> I told Asegret Bertha that what the Ethiopian government said was a lie. The conflict that happened between the Anywaa and Nuer was in 2001 and 2002 during the presidency of Okello Nyigelo. The people who were involved, including the former president Okello Nyigelo, were put in federal prison. But this time, it was the federal forces that were killing civilians because of the incident that happened on the way to Odier. Without knowing the people who ambushed the car, the federal forces started killing Anywaa people in Gambella town and Anywaa villages. There are so many armed groups around Gambella area such as SPLA, OLF, Nuer, and Opwo. I don't know why they singled out the Anywaa people, and even had a list of names of the most educated Anywaa men to be killed. I told her that the numbers of the victims were still unknown, and that the dogs started feeding on the bodies lying on the streets. We could hear hyenas, they were feeding on the dead bodies outside the town, and those who died in the bush. I told her that Gambella was in darkness.[16]

The interview that Okello Akway had with the Germans was released the following day in the afternoon, and it was very different from the report that Dr. Gebre-Aba Barnabas gave on December 15. During the same night of December 15, Obang Metho[17] connected with Genocide Watch and

16. Interview with Okello Akway (August 29, 2022).

17. Activist Obang Metho struggled to make the Anywaa genocide known to the world. Mr. Obang Metho reached out to Human Rights Watch during the Anywaa genocide of 2003. In 2013, activist Obang Metho testified in the White House in Washington, D.C., at the US Congressional Briefing on Land Grabs in Africa and described the atrocities the Anywaa faced in Ethiopia. He was the founder and executive director of the Solidarity Movement for a New Ethiopia (SMNE).

had them call Okello Akway and interview him. Doug McGill, a former New York Times reporter, was the first person to report about the Anywaa genocide on his website, The McGill Report. His report brought the Anywaa genocide to international attention and put the first pressure on PM Meles Zenawi and the Ethiopian government. After Okello Akway's interviews were released by the Germans, the international community increased the pressure on the government of Ethiopia.

Dr. Gebre-Aba Barnabas was then sent to Gambella by the federal government. Okello Akway said:

> I was not informed that Dr. Gebre-Aba Barnabas was coming to Gambella. I just heard it from someone who was close to me. I went to the airport that day to receive him, but Omod Obang and Tsegaye were already there waiting for him.[18]

When Dr. Gebre-Aba Barnabas arrived, he went to Omod and Tsegaye and sent one of the security guards to Okello to tell him that he could lead the way. Okello Akway told his driver to take them to the Ethiopia Hotel. When they got to the hotel, Alma Alamorum was already there. Dr. Gebre-Aba Barnabas had a program with him that was laid out by the federal government. The first thing that he asked was to send the elders to Pinyudo and get the situation there under control. At that time, all the Anywaa men from different villages were gathered in Pinyudo fighting the federal forces in the area, while thousands of Anywaa women, elders, and children were using that route to escape to Pochala, South Sudan. Okello Akway gave him a list of people: Omod Agwa, pastor Daku Okon, Omod Opiew (Ogwol), and Otwier Ojho. When those elders got to Pinyudo, they met the young people there who defended the area, and they were already there to defend themselves, their people, and their land. Things were very different in Pinyudo, and the number of victims were low because of this resistance by the youths, while in Gambella so many people died, houses burnt, and thousands of people escaped to forests. The December 13, 2003 genocide first became known internationally on The McGill Report, a website written by Doug McGill, a former New York Times reporter living in Minnesota. He published the story one week after December 13, based on cellphone interviews with eyewitnesses in Gambella to the massacre, and by interviewing Anywaa refugees in Minnesota who had spoken by cellphone to family members and friends in Gambella, as the massacre was actually happening.

---

18. Interview with Okello Akway (August 29, 2022).

Few meetings took place in Gambella, and the killing stopped in the town. During these meetings, the Anywaa people made it clear that the federal government was the one that carried out the killing in Gambella. People like Okok, who was a judge, and Juu Kwot, who was a soldier, asked Dr. Gebre-Aba Barnabas in the Ethiopia hotel about who gave the order to kill the Anywaa civilians in their lands. Dr. Gebre-Aba Barnabas tried to deny the involvement of the federal government, stating that the order was not to kill the Anywaa civilians. According to Okello Akway, a person named Colonel Ethiopia came from Jimma with his soldiers, and he was carrying the spirits of Ethiopianism. He was from the Amhara ethnic group. He called me at my office, and asked how he could help with his soldiers. Okello Akway said:

> I told Colonel Ethiopia to meet me in the morning, and I asked him to help rebuild the houses that were burnt.[19]

Over four hundred houses were burnt down in Gambella town alone, and thousands of people hid in the forests. Colonel Ethiopia and his soldiers helped with the reconstructions, the Anywaa people who were hiding in forests were called to come back home, and the regional government provided one hundred thousand *birr* to buy mosquito nets and other materials for cooking since everything was burned down. This was the second week of the genocide. The houses that were built by the federal forces were poorly built and not suitable for living. Hence, most of them were never used by the Anywaa survivors who returned.

Dr. Gebre-Aba Barnabas brought people with him to do their own investigation about the genocide that they have committed on the Anywaa people. The federal government gave this responsibility to Dr. Gebre-Aba Barnabas as they faced more pressure from the international community. The investigators he brought were stationed next to the office of the president. Okello Akway said:

> The people that they interviewed were the wives of the Anywaa men who were members of the EPRDF. None of their husbands were killed because they were placed at the Grand Hotel where they were protected. I asked them why they were interviewing the women because the targeted people were Anywaa men. Also, none

---

19. Okello Akway (August 29, 2022)

of the women's husbands that they were interviewing were killed since they worked for the government.[20]

This fake selective investigation did not make any progress. It was another attempt to change the reality of what took place in Gambella and erase the involvement of the federal government in the Anywaa genocide.

At the end of two weeks, Dr. Gebre-Aba Barnabas and a group of people from the Nuer, Anywaa, Opwo, Majang, Komo, Air Forces, and other securities went to the president's office, and Dr. Gebre-Aba Barnabas demanded that president Okello Akway change his statement to Genocide Watch and to German radio. This is what Okello Akway said to them:

> I made it clear to them that there is nothing I could change about my statement because that was what happened. I told them that if they could bring back the dead people to live and I see them with my own eyes walking and talking, then I can tell the German radio and Genocide Watch that the dead people came back to live.[21]

Dr. Gebre-Aba Barnabas understood that there was no way that President Okello Akway would change his mind or change his statement about the Anywaa genocide. Three weeks later, he brought his own journalists to Gambella and sent them to president Okello Akway. He told Okello Akway that he could talk freely about what happened. According to Okello Akway, he told them about what happened and made it clear that what happened in Gambella constituted genocide and crimes against humanity. The journalists and Dr. Gebre-Aba Barnabas went back to Addis Ababa without getting what he wanted, which was to take the blame off the Ethiopian government and had Okello Akway changed the statement he gave to German radio and Genocide Watch. They couldn't do anything to Okello Akway either because he still had his immunity, so they waited until he was removed from his position and had no immunity. After they went back to Addis Ababa, the interview of Okello Akway and Tsegaye Beyene was released. But they only had the picture of Okello Akway in the newspaper and all the things he said during his interview were not included in the paper. On the other hand, Tsegaye Beyene's interview was on the same newspaper where he said:

---

20. Okello Akway (August 29, 2022)
21. Interview with Okello Akway (August 29, 2022).

The Anywaa Genocide

> If anyone blames the incident that took place in Gambella on the Ethiopian government and Meles Zenawi, he is the enemy, and we will take action on him.[22]

On January 7th, 2004, in the afternoon, there was a meeting that took place in Gambella at *Mikir Bet*. The Ethiopian government officials who were at the meeting included Tsegaye Beyene, Alma Alamorum, and Getachew Asefa. The Ginbar Party[23] was leading the meeting, and President Okello Akway represented the Congress Party. The chairmen of the Ginbar Party were Keet Twac (from the Nuer ethnic group), Omod Obang Olom (an Anywaa), and Weynetu Abera (from the Majang tribe). The points that were raised during the meeting were to put all the blame on the regional leadership. That was when Okello Akway raised his hand and said:

> Everything you all said about the regional leadership was right. If everything that happened in Gambella was because of bad leadership, then the TPLF is responsible for everything because they are the ones running Gambella.[24]

Everyone became quiet at the meeting. President Okello Akway said that because Gambella is always run by the federal government, not the local government. The regional officials just follow what they are told to do and not to do. The chairmen then started to blame what happened on the conflict between the Anywaa and Nuer. Again, Okello Akway made it clear that what happened between the Anywaa and Nuer was in 2001, and people like Okello Nyigelo were put in prison for it. The meeting was then rushed through so that the people at the meeting would rule out by raising hands that what happened in Gambella was a tribal conflict between the Anywaa and Nuer. Everything ended when Okello Akway raised his hand and said:

> From now on, I will not meet about anything related to the Anywaa genocide unless there is a third party at the meeting.[25]

The people who were leading the meeting then stood up and said, "The meeting is done!" The Mikir Bet compound was surrounded by the highlanders, including people like Agere Eshetu who was involved in the Anywaa killings as well. After the meeting, Okello Akway went to his house,

---

22. Interview with Okello Akway (August 29, 2022).

23. The Ginbar Party represented the party that ruled Ethiopia after overthrowing the Derg government.

24. Interview with Okello Akway (August 29, 2022).

25. Interview with Okello Akway (August 29, 2022).

and Tsegaye's team went to the Ethiopia Hotel for another meeting. The agenda of the meeting was to create a report that says that the government of Ethiopia only killed fifty-nine men and one woman during the incident, and then have the president agree and sign. If Okello Akway refused to sign the report, then he would be removed from his position and killed. The person who signed this order was Abay Tsehaye, who was the minister of federal affairs and an executive member of the Central Committee of the TPLF Party at that time. On the night of January 7, 2004, Cwol Bich, one of the Nuer who was not at the meeting but heard about it, called Okello Akway at around 11 p.m. and said, "President Okello Akway, why are you still in Gambella? Your era is over."[26] Cwol Bich was warning Okello Akway that he needed to leave Gambella because Abay Tsehaye already signed an order that he should be killed if he did not cooperate.

On January 8, at 7 a.m., Okello Akway went to his office to collect some of his documents and his money that he had not collected yet from his accountant. Then he gave the car keys to his driver Ngadhe Ojulu, who was released from the jail and drove back home. Okello Akway gave his wife some money, and he went on his way to Pochala, South Sudan, without telling anyone, including his wife. Okello Akway said:

> When we passed Abwobo around 8:15 a.m., I told my driver to take the car back to Gambella, and then meet me in Pochala because he wanted to go with me.[27]

Okello Akway slept in Pokedi and then reached Pochala the next day on January 9, 2003. Thousands of Anywaa people, including women and children, were already relocated in Pochala, South Sudan at that time. Professor Gregory Stanton sent the first international investigative team to Gambella, from Genocide Watch, after learning more about the Anywaa genocide from The McGill Report website. According to Okello Akway, the Anywaa genocide was well planned out by the TPLF government after the discovery of oil in the Anywaa land in Jor woreda. The agreement was signed between the TPLF government, and a Chinese contractor called China's Zhongyuan Petroleum Exploration Bureau and Malaysia's state-owned oil corporation (Petronas). The construction of the road from Tigray passing through Benishangul region went into effect after the agreement was signed. Okello Akway stated:

26. Interview with Okello Akway (August 29, 2022).
27. Interview with Okello Akway (August 29, 2022).

The Anywaa Genocide

On September 24, 2003, a group of eleven people met in the office of prime minister and planned out the Anywaa genocide. They signed the paper for the Anywaa genocide this day, and the reason was for the oil in Jor woreda. The eleven people who signed the paper were Meles Zenawi, Addisu Legesse, Bereket Simon, Samora Yunis, Yohannes Gebremeskel, Abadula Gemeda, Abay Tsehaye, Dr. Gebre-Aba Barnabas, Almaw Alemeraw, Sibhat Nega, and Tadesse HaileSelase. The other three people who were involved in the killing on the ground were Omod Obang Olom, Tsegaye Beyene, and Shambel Amare.[28]

During this meeting at the office of prime minister, 762 names of educated Anywaa men were written down. The names were written down by Omod Obang Olom per Prime Minister Meles Zenawi's request, and he was promised that he would become the president of Gambella. The plan was that during the first wave of killing, 512 men would be killed. Then 250 would be killed in the second round. Okello Akway said:

> My name was among the 250 people; I was supposed to be killed on the second round of killing.[29]

---

28. Interview with Okello Akway (August 29, 2022).
29. Interview with Okello Akway (August 29, 2022).

Anywaa | Part 3

Former president of Gambella Mr. Okello Akway was born in a small village in Thatha called Diipa on March 12, 1962 E.C., Okello Akway attended American missionary school in Pinyudo through third grade. When he got to fourth grade, he had to go to Akado because Emperor Haile Selassie allowed the school in Pinyudo to be from first to third grade only. School in Akado was allowed till sixth grade. In 1964 E.C, school was opened to sixth grade in Ya-Ageenga (Pinyudo). After he finished sixth grade, he went to Abwobo for school and then to Dembidolo and finished eighth and ninth grade. Okello came back to Gambella and finished his high school at Gambella High school. After high school, he went to Nekemte and got his diploma in Nursing. Okello Akway came back to Gambella and worked for several years and became the director of the healthcare bureau. Then, he went to Jimma and studied public health for his bachelor's degree. He also got an opportunity to study at Black Lion medical facility in Addis Ababa. Before going to Addis Ababa for school, Okello Akway was a member of the Congress political party in Gambella. When Okello Nyigelo was removed from his position, Okello Akway was temporarily appointed to be the president of Gambella. Okello Akway served for nine months before he left the region after the Dec 13, 2003, Anywaa genocide. Okello is married to Adwuo Omod Oboo, and he has four kids with her who are residing in Norway; he has two kids in North America; and he has two kids in Gambella. His mother's name is Abwola Oliek or Abwolla Nyookiio.

Chapter 10

The Crimes against Humanity

THE ANYWAA PEOPLE WERE already being oppressed by the Derg government, but it got worse under the leadership of the TPLF government. Anywaa land has natural resources such as water, fertile land, petroleum (oil and gas), gold, platinum, and tungsten. According to the joint field report by Genocide Watch and Survivors' Rights International on February 25, 2004, "Today is the Day of Killing Anuaks," the treatment of the Anywaa people by the Ethiopian government got worse since oil was discovered under Anywaa lands by the Gambella Petroleum Corporation, a subsidiary of Pinewood Resources Ltd. of Canada, which signed a concession agreement with the Ethiopian government in 2001. After Pinewood announced that it had relinquished all rights to the Gambella oil concession, Malaysia's state-owned petroleum corporation, Petronas, signed an agreement on June 13, 2003, with the EPRDF government to exploit the Ogaden Basin and the Gambella Block.[1] The Anywaa people started to get worried after the discovery of these resources in Gambella because they knew what was coming. It didn't take very long, the government of Ethiopia started disarming the Anywaa police, followed by the genocide of December 13, 2003.

On December 13, 2003, the Anywaa people were brutally massacred in Gambella town and the villages around it. The Anywaa were killed using machetes, knives, rocks, sticks, hoes, axes, and bullets when they tried to escape. Some were burned alive inside their hut houses, thrown into the river with their arms tied in their backs, or run over with military trucks.

1. "'Today is the Day of Killing Anuaks.'"

Women were gang raped, including young girls and older women. Some women were raped in front of their husbands, before their husbands were killed. In this chapter, I put together different stories from people who went through and barely survived the genocide.

This was the darkest day that the Anywaa people had ever faced before in their history. I still remember it very well. It was Saturday morning on December 13, 2003. A normal Saturday but much quieter than usual days. The birds were not chirping like usual, and it was a slightly cloudy and chilly morning. Like any other morning, my mother was sweeping our little compound while the men at our house were brushing their teeth. I was outside waiting for breakfast, which was tea and bread. That is when I heard three gunshots followed by a long silence. Then heard my mother saying in Dha-Anywaa *"mor bee kuuwe mo opooti mac obeede!"* meaning that "it might be the usual shootings at the thieves!" People were already used to Anywaa young men getting shot in the town and being labeled as *shifta* or thief. But this one was different. A few minutes later, there was loud screaming and cries that grew from a distance. The screaming grew louder and louder and followed by more gunshots that we had never heard before. It sounded like the gunshots in American war movies that I was familiar with. That was when my mother picked up my little brother, then grabbed my hand and we rushed into our living room with everyone else in our home. The gunshots never stopped after that.

More and more people from our neighborhood came to our house to hide, and then many people from Omiininga arrived. More than fifty people filled our bedroom and the veranda. The people from Omiininga then told us that the Anywaa men were targeted and that *gaale* (meaning the Highlanders) and the soldiers in uniform were also burning down the Anywaa houses. The men in our room were hiding under the bed, and the kids were sitting on the bed. I could see the fear in the adult's eyes; some were crying and others praying. As time went on, the room got hotter and hotter since there was no air conditioner inside. They had no choice but to open the windows; the kids also started crying nonstop because of the heat and hunger, and their mother would take them outside and sit in front of the door. Whenever the gunshots got louder, they would run back inside and then go back outside when gunshots reduced. The men only got out from under the bed to get water and take fresh air, and then get back under the bed. The children only ate that day; we were given *keewa* (an Anywaa food made of corn flour and mixed with groundnuts). The adults didn't eat anything. The soldiers skipped our neighborhood in Addis Sefer and continued with the killing at Tier Kidi, going from door to door of the Anywaa people. There were not many killings that took place in Addis Safer because the highlanders in our neighborhood stood up and protected the neighborhood from those Highlanders who were involved in the killing and looting. They (some highlanders) took some Anywaa people and hid them in their houses. So many Anywaa men survived in such ways. Hundreds of women and children from Omiininga ran to the Mekane Yesus compound for hiding, including some young men who survived. A young man named Ato Kimo helped open the Mekane Yesus compound's gate, and hundreds of people from Omiininga entered the compound.

On this day, the Highlanders and the Ethiopian federal forces worked together to massacre, rape, and torture the defenseless Anywaa people on their land. The systematic use of rape as a weapon against the Anywaa women was meant to destroy the Anywaa ethnic group and resulted in pregnancy with mixed children. Regional police officers recorded 138 cases of Anywaa women being raped in Gambella town alone, all in the month of December 2003.[2] In Anywaa culture, rape is one of the worst crimes that someone can commit. The victim will have to live with the trauma for the rest of their life. If the victim is not married yet, no Anywaa man from that area will ever marry the victim unless they move to a different village where their story of rape is not known. If the woman is married, the husband might do anything to the man who raped their wife, even killing him. So, there were so many rapes that were committed by the Ethiopian forces and the Highlanders on the Anywaa women that were not reported by the victims due to these strong social taboos. All the rapes that took place were gang rapes that involved at least three perpetrators. Some of the rapes involved teenagers and little girls. According to the Genocide Watch and Survivors' Rights International Field Report in 2004, a thirteen-year-old was raped in Ye-cwaay village on December 20, and five girls (ages twelve, fourteen, sixteen, seventeen, and twenty) were raped in Gambella town. One of the most heartbreaking evil acts occurred on January 28, 2004. A ten-year-old daughter was gang raped in front of her father by EPRDF soldiers. When the father attempted to challenge the soldiers, he was executed by the soldiers. On the same day in Pinyudo, a fifteen-year-old girl was also raped by six EPRDF soldiers. After being raped, she went home and

---

2. "Today is the Day of Killing Anuaks."

committed suicide.³ The raping of Anywaa girls was deliberately carried out to prevent them from having children in the future. During this dark time, Anywaa women were living in fear for themselves and their daughters; the men were defenseless and could not say anything because the punishment for speaking out or saying anything would be death or torture that would result in death later.

The Anywaa men are known to be very protective of their women, children, and their relatives. There is an Anywaa saying that if you want to get beaten by a coward, try to fight them when their woman is around. During the genocide, the Anywaa men in Gambella town became like women; they couldn't do anything to defend themselves or their women. Some men survived because they wore women's dresses, and the soldiers thought that they were women. Gang raping Anywaa women and killing Anywaa men by the soldiers became a norm in the Anywaa villages. Many women also committed suicide after being gang raped. On December 22, 2003, the soldiers entered Ajulu Ogula's home in Abwobo district looking for her husband. When they couldn't find him, they gang raped Ajulu Ogula and then killed her at her house. Sometimes, the soldiers deliberately used rapes to send a message to the Anywaa men that they (the soldiers) are in charge and could do anything that they wanted. One of the stories reported by Genocide Watch and Survivors' Rights International clearly showed how cruel and immoral the EPRDF soldiers were. On December 15, 2003, a forty-three-year-old woman in Eleya village was gang raped just in front of her husband and two children. The father couldn't do anything because he would be killed if he tried to.⁴ Hundreds of rapes that occurred in Gambella town, Abwobo, Pinyudo, Itang, Dimma, Jor, and small Anywaa villages around Gambella never get reported by the victims due to the shame and humiliation that comes with it. Most of these rapes resulted in pregnancies with mixed children, which was one of the intentions of using rape as a weapon. The other intention was to infect as many of Anywaa women with HIV/AIDS to cause more death in the future. In the 2005 Ethiopia demographic and health surveys (EDHS), the overall prevalence of HIV in Ethiopia was 1.4 percent, and Gambella had the highest prevalence in the entire country at 6 percent, followed by Addis Ababa at 4.7 percent.⁵ Within Gambella, the largest Anywaa cities like Pignudo, Gambella town,

---

3. *"Today is the Day of Killing Anuaks."*
4. *"Today is the Day of Killing Anuaks."*
5. Kibret et al., "Trends and Spatial Distributions of HIV," 3.

The Crimes Against Humanity

and Dimma had the highest prevalence of HIV. The systemic use of rape as a weapon had gradually caused many deaths in the Anywaa community because of HIV/AIDS.

Anywaa men endured unspeakable torture during and after the genocide. This torture was deliberately carried out by EPRDF soldiers to punish, intimidate, and obtain information about the most wanted Anywaa men, including the former president of Gambella, Okello Akway. Among those who were tortured, jailed, or killed included those who were suspected of being *shifta* or who collaborated with the Anywaa militias that were using the guerilla war to fight Ethiopian forces. Hundreds if not thousands of Anywaa men were kept in prison where they were intimidated, tortured, and even disappeared (killed). In many cases of these tortures and beatings, the Anywaa men were continuously kicked or hit with the butt of a weapon in their private parts. This was mainly to make sure that they won't be able to reproduce if they survive. The Genocide Watch and Survivors' Rights International reported one of the cases as follows:

> One of the most egregious cases is that of the illegal arrest, detention, and torture of Othow Akway Ochalla, the brother of the President of Gambella, Okello Akway Ochalla. Mr. Ochalla was last seen on January 27, 2004, by an eyewitness who visited him in prison and reported that Mr. Ochalla had been tortured: his body and head were swollen, he was coughing blood, and he believed that he would not survive. Further requests to visit Mr. Ochalla have been denied, and it is believed by many that he has died. Family members of surviving prisoners have been allowed visitations, but many people have not been seen since they were arrested. During daylight hours, Anuak prisoners are subject to forced labor under armed guard and are reportedly forced to cut trees and rebuild dwellings incinerated or otherwise destroyed during the December pogrom.[6]

---

6. "Today is the Day of Killing Anuaks."

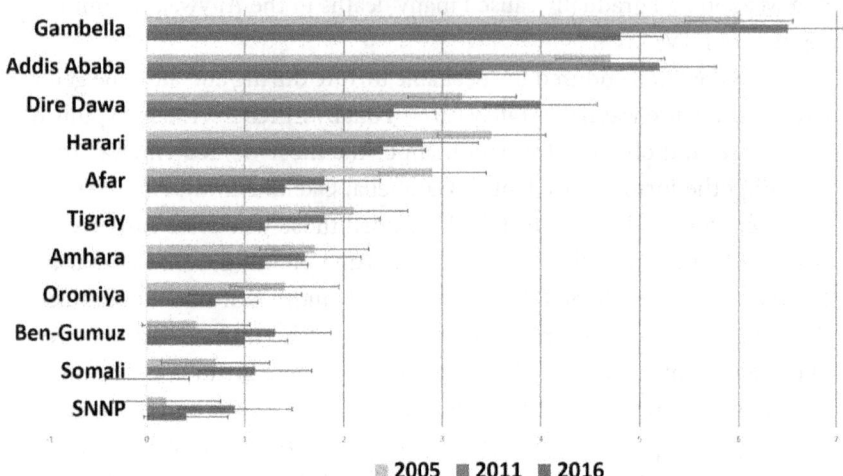

Trends of HIV by region; data from EDHS 2005, 2011, and 2016.[7]

---

7. Kibret et al., "Trends and Spatial Distributions of HIV," 4.

Chapter 11

Revenge against the EPRDF

THE GUERILLA WARS THAT the Anywaa people fought against the government forces had opened a corridor from Pinyudo to Pochala, South Sudan. This corridor was used by thousands of Anywaa people to escape to South Sudan. Among the heroes who fought to protect the Anywaa people who were fleeing the genocide were Ngeeli Oliru, Kwot Agid and his brother Bare Agid, and Ochang Okello. During the day of genocide on December 13, 2003, one of the first Anywaa heroes who responded in Pinyudo and fought the federal forces who arrived in Pinyudo was Commander Ngeeli Oliru. I want to dedicate this part of the book to one of the Anywaa heroes, who sacrificed his life to protect his people and his ancestral lands: Commander Ngeeli Oliru. During the time of my interview with Ngeeli Oliru on August 31, 2022, he was between thirty-seven to forty years old. Ngeeli Oliru was born and grew up in a small village called Chienthoa, located in Jor woreda. When he was a child, Ngeeli lost his parents and became an orphan. He was then raised by his stepmother, second wife of his father, and supported by his uncle. His biological mother's name is Olammi, and his uncle's name is Lwaal Ojwato. The stepmother who raised him is Okwar Ochala. Ngeeli had two other siblings. At the age of 18, Ngeeli Oliru joined the Ethiopian National Defense Forces and served his country. He fought during the war of Badme, and he was shot four times in the battle. During his stay on the war front, Ngeeli was with other Anywaa people named Othow Omod (from Gog woreda) and Ochala Gebriel from Abol woreda. He also met people like Ataale, Kobi, and Kaunda Oman on the war front.

On June 10, 1999, Ngeeli Oliru was shot during the war at the Battle of Barentu. On May 12, 2000, he caught another three bullets in his legs at the battle of Mereb-Setit. Ngeeli Oliru was finally dismissed from his duty in June 2003 when he fought the soldiers in his camp and killed seven of them.

On December 13, 2003, Ngeeli Oliru was staying in Pinyudo. When the ENDF reached Pinyudo, they started killing and burning down houses on day one. The people fled to the forests and small villages nearby. The Anywaa police started resisting with the few weapons they had and allowed women, children, and elders to escape to the little villages closer to Pinyudo. Ngeeli Oliru, Okony Okoth, Oduru Omod, and a few other young men then organized themselves and counterattacked the ENDF in Pinyudo on December 14, 2003. They fought the whole day, killing many federal forces who arrived in Pinyudo. The ENDF called for more reinforcement from Gambella town as they suffered high casualties and deaths. When the first asylum seekers reached Pochala, South Sudan, people like Obang Kut and Ogaami picked up their guns and went to Pinyudo to join the people who were already resisting. When they arrived in Pinyudo, they joined the fight. This resistance was to keep the Pochala corridor open for the Anywaa people to escape to South Sudan without the federal forces hunting them down. Thousands of Anywaa people fled to Pochala, while the federal forces faced a very tough resistance from the Anywaa fighters in Pinyudo town. Then, Ngeeli and his team retreated to Pochala after the elders were sent to Pinyudo to stop the fighting over there. Ngeeli Oliru was shot in the foot during the fights in Pinyudo, but he could still walk. Ngeeli Oliru stated:

> When we retreated to Pochala, South Sudan, we had a meeting with our fighters and all the new young people who were willing to join us and defend the Anywaa people and lands. We then divided the Anywaa lands between the teams: the Obang Kut and Ochan team would go to Dimma woreda; Okello Chek's team, Kwot Agid's team, and my team took on Teedo (an all Baat-Gilo area) and Baat-Openo lands. Since most of the people on our team were not soldiers, we started training them in the Jor woreda area because it is open land and showed them the technique of fighting. Among those who were veterans from ENDF were me, Omod Otook, Omod Ogwok, Oloch Obirri, and Wataga from Gog.[1]

---

1. Interview with Commander Ngeeli Oliru (August 31, 2022).

Revenge against the EPRDF

When President Okello Akway escaped, Ngeeli's team went to Teedo and took Okello Akway to Pochala. On their stay in Pochala, Southern Sudan, the Anywaa people prepared to take revenge on the Ethiopian government forces. Those young men were the survivors of the genocide, and some of them barely escaped the killing. Different groups were organized to go back to Ethiopia and take revenge. Young people who lost their parents, their loved ones, and those who were brutally beaten and escaped, and even the Anywaa of Pochala, Southern Sudan, who felt the pain of their Anywaa people joined the groups and came back to Ethiopia to fight with guerrilla warfare. The team in Dimma woreda opened the first attack on January 29, 2004, and defeated the EPRDF forces in Dimma.[2] The Anywaa militants seized more weapons from the Ethiopian government forces, and over 160 people died during that attack. After the attack, the EPRDF responded by jailing an estimated 150–300 Anywaa people on February 2, 2004. Anywaa civilians were tortured by the EPRDF forces to give information about the Anywaa militia or show their location. The tortures involved beating with the butts of guns until many of them started vomiting blood, laying them down naked in the sun for hours on their stomachs, and denying them water and food for days. When the president of Gambella, Okello Akway, escaped to Pochala, Southern Sudan, some people were arrested and beaten to show the location of the president. On February 3, 2004, the EPRDF forces killed over forty Anywaa civilians in Dimma. The names of the sixteen Anywaa civilians who were killed in the Dimma massacre on February 3, 2004, and recorded by the Genocide Watch and Survivors' Rights International Field Report were Owar Okongo, Ochong Aballa, Alwoch, Oman Ogatu, Badok Obang, Omod Ojaye, Ojila Ochala, Odola Opiew, Omod Onele, John Ajaak, Ojine Omod, James Omod, Okok Ojulu, Opap Owar, Cham Omod Nyengori, and Odoong Abela. The names of the wounded were Otonge Okello, Omod Oman, Donagatache Okuch, Ojulu Adong, and Opiew Owile.

The team led by Ngeeli Oliru opened an attack on the federal forces in Pokedi village in the month of February 2004. After they successfully destroyed the forces in Pokedi, they went on and fought in Okuna. Ngeeli Oliru described the war as follows:

> The number of federal forces in Okuna was overwhelming, so we retreated and went back to Baat-Gilo. The federal forces followed us to Baat-Gilo, and we fought them again and retreated to a place

---

2. "Today is the Day of Killing Anuaks."

called Buur Anger. The Ethiopian forces were using some Anywaa traitors to show our locations. So, they came to Buur Anger, and we fought there as well. During the war of Buur Anger, we ran out of ammunition, so Kwot Agid went to Pochala, South Sudan, to bring ammunition, and he came back with someone named Otwier Ochala and Omod Othoo, who was a soldier as well.[3]

When Kwot Agid brought ammunition from Pochala, they met in a place called Aau. The federal forces arrived in Aau following the Anywaa fighters, and they fought in this area. According to Ngeeli, the battle of Aau was one of the longest battles they had. It was at this time when Kwot Agid became too tired and couldn't run around anymore. Kwot Agid was the oldest and the most experienced fighter in the group. Ngeeli Oliru said:

> The fighting got more intense as the Ethiopian government kept sending more forces and increasing the numbers. Kwot Agid was almost captured by the enemies in this battle because he couldn't run around anymore. We couldn't leave him behind because he was the oldest and the most experienced and a great GPLM fighter in our team. So, we stayed and sacrificed our lives to keep him alive. We decided that it would be much better that some of us die to keep him alive. Some people carried him, while most of us were fighting a great number of federal forces. We were outnumbered, but we managed to open a way out and sent Kwot Agid to a small village called Ojala. Our forces then went to Chienthoa village where we were followed by the Ethiopian forces again. During the battle of Chienthoa, we lost two older fighters: Akwuiy, and I forgot the name of the other person. My cousin Ochala was wounded in this battle. After the battle of Chienthoa, we retreated and went to Kwot Agid, then we moved to Jor and stayed there where the oil was discovered. As we expected, the Anywaa traitors brought the federal forces to our area, and we fought at the battle of Orang. We lost two people in this war: Opwola and Atiedo; they were cousins. A person named Ojulu was shot and wounded in his hand, and Omod Agii was shot in his private area. After a long fight, we retreated and went to Gilo's side. We stayed there for the night, and in the morning, we fought the federal forces again, and another warrior Obach Omooro died. During all these wars, the numbers of federal forces who died were very high. Whenever we finished up one team, another team would arrive. They just kept

---

3. Interview with Commander Ngeeli Oliru (August 31, 2022).

coming and coming in large numbers, and we kept fighting and changing locations.[4]

During the rainy season around April and May of 2004, Ngeeli and his team went to Omiila. When they were on their way to Omiila, the Ethiopian forces went to Teedo and fought with Girma Ojulu's team, and Girma lost five of his fighters while causing a devastating loss to the Ethiopian forces. By the time that Ngeeli's team arrived in Omiila, the South Sudanese already had an agreement with the Ethiopian government. According to Ngeeli Oliru, Obang Kut and his team were already converted and were working with the SPLM. The SPLM forces took thirty weapons from Ngeeli's team at that time. This was the beginning of destroying the relationship of the Anywaa teams who were at the beginning working together to take revenge on the government of Ethiopia. When it became impossible to stay in Pochala, Ngeeli Oliru and eleven other people left Pochala and went to Murle's village in Pibor. This was around June of 2004. People who left with Ngeeli included Kwot Agid, Bare Agid, Onyongngo Akway, Okello Ojulu, Ochan Akway, and Ojha. Ngeeli Oliru said:

> The Murle people welcomed us, provided food for us, and gave us a refugee camp to stay in.[5]

Many Anywaa refugees followed and joined them in Pibor refugee camp. According to Ngeeli, the Anywaa administration in Pochala worked with the government of Sudan to prevent any armed Anywaa group from staying in Pochala, and among the people who were involved was the administrator of Pochala, Ogatu.

On July 2, 2004, Ngeeli and his team went back to Pochala to take the rest of his team members that were still staying there. When they arrived in Otaalo, Obang Oluuc, Ochang Okello, and SPLA soldiers fought them, and two people from Ngeeli's side were wounded, whereas one person died on the Ochang Okello side. Ngeeli and his team went back to Pibor camp, and they had a meeting about whether they should attack Pochala or not. Ngeeli Oliru stated:

> During the meeting, we decided to go and attack Pochala and kill them all. But we didn't proceed with that plan because we were all Anywaa. Even if we go and attack Pochala, the people from the other side were still Anywaa people and we were fighting to take

4. Interview with Commander Ngeeli Oliru (August 31, 2022).
5. Interview with Commander Ngeeli Oliru (August 31, 2022).

revenge on the Ethiopian government for killing us on our lands. The other Anywaa who resided with the SPLM were just doing that for money. So, we decided not to attack Pochala[6]

In 2005, Ngeeli Oliru and thirty-eight other people went from Pibor refugee camp to a place called Yith-Boole and opened a new base there to keep fighting with the Ethiopian government. It became very challenging for them to keep fighting due to lack of ammunition. So, they went back to the camp in Pibor and decided to send Kwot Agid and Otwier Ochala to go to Eritrea to obtain weapons and ammunition. In July 2005, Kwot Agid was captured by the government of Sudan at a place called Kassala on his way to Khartoum to get to Eritrea. He was then handed over to the government of Ethiopia and was taken to the federal prison in Addis Ababa. After the capture of Kwot Agid, there was a division that took place in the camp among the fighters. Some people wanted to go back to Pochala and join the people over there, and others wanted to go to Eritrea. Ngeeli's team kept searching for alliances to get weapons and ammunition and continued the guerilla warfare with the Ethiopian government. They then tried to make an alliance with some rebel groups who were fighting the TPLF at that time. They met a person called Getu Molla and Asgidu and went to Khartoum in 2006. After coming back from Khartoum, they connected with Obang Medho in the United States. The relationship did not last very long. Ngeeli Oliru said:

> *Gaale* (referring to the highlanders) started bragging about the Anywaa people that they killed in Gambella. They used to be a part of ENDF, and some of them were in Gambella and participated in the Anywaa genocide. They were saying that they participated in the killings because they wanted the Anywaa to hate the TPLF government and eventually join the struggle against the government. Getu Molla who was a former Shambel of ENDF said that he killed about twenty-four Anywaa in Pinyudo and buried them in a mass grave.[7]

This created a conflict, and Ngeeli killed them, including their leader Getu Molla. This incident made it unsafe for Ngeeli Oliru to stay in Sudan, and he was allowed by the Ethiopian government to come back to Ethiopia since he killed the leaders of the Amhara rebels including Getu Molla. On his arrival in Gambella, Ngeeli Oliru was appointed as the leader of regional militias by Omod Obang.

6. Interview with Commander Ngeeli Oliru (August 31, 2022).
7. Interview with Commander Ngeeli Oliru (August 31, 2022).

Revenge against the EPRDF

Ngeeli was accepted back in Ethiopia, and the federal government wanted to promote him at the federal government, but he chose to stay in Gambella. Ngeeli Oliru said:

> I wanted to work for my people and anything that concerns the Anywaa land. I was then appointed as the leader of the militias in Jor woreda.[8]

In May 2007, the regional special forces were created, and Ngeeli Oliru became their leader and a trainer. After giving training to the first round of the special forces for four months, he worked in Gambella town as one of the special forces' heads. In Jor woreda there was a federal security officer who was Tigrayan, and he also worked as a shopkeeper. According to Ngeeli, he mentioned to him one day that he played a role in the Anywaa genocide, and Ngeeli Oliru killed him right away. Ngeeli was then put in prison for the killing of that security for one year and three months. After serving one year and three months going to the fourth month, Ngeeli escaped the prison in 2011. Ngeeli went to South Sudan and met the Anywaa groups who wanted to keep fighting the Ethiopian government. In the same year, Ngeeli and his team went and attacked the federal forces in Jor, Gog, and in the Oromia region. Ngeeli Oliru was leading the group organized by Okello Akway, and there was another group organized by Aballa Obang and led by Omod Odol, who was an American citizen. The struggle became very challenging when the government of South Sudan tightened up their diplomatic relationship with the government of Ethiopia. So, Ngeeli and his team decided to go back to the refugee camp, but they were captured by the Sudanese government and handed over to the government of Ethiopia. Omod Ojulu Odol stayed in Ethiopia fighting the TPLF government where he was killed with five other Anywaa men. According to Mr. Ochala Abulla, the Chairman of Anywaa Justice, Omod Odol, was killed while he was sitting under a tree with sixteen other people: Gogo Ochalla, Cham Ochalla, Okach Achaw, Akway Omod, Omod Obang, Agaba Akway, Omod Ojulu Oguta, Abacha Ojulu, Thole Olok, Ochwal Obang, Owar Cham, Nyimolo Agola, Aberach Nyimolo, Akonya Omod, Agwa Cham, Owar Nyigwo, and a number of children as young as ten years of age. They were sitting under the shade of a tree at the bank of Gilo River when the ENDF arrived and opened fire at them, killing six people, including an eleven-year-old boy.

---

8. Interview with Commander Ngeeli Oliru (August 31, 2022).

After the death of Omod Odol, his pictures and his American passport were reported throughout Ethiopia using government-controlled media and news channels. They took the body of Omod Odol to Pinyudo and drove his body tied on the top of an army truck, showing and displaying it to the Anywaa people in the town. As they drove his body around, they were shouting, screaming in joy and telling people that the most wanted terrorist is dead, the man who was "anti-foreign investment" and "anti-villagization." Omod Ojulu Odol was killed on March 2, 2013, along with five other people. On March 3, the regional government planned to bring the body of Omod Odol to Gambella and drove him around the city just like they did in Pinyudo. Before they brought his body to Gambella town, the federal government stopped them, warning that it might anger the public and lead to unrest in the town. The diplomatic approach by the Ethiopian government and South Sudan led to the capturing of Ngeeli and his team in 2012, and the death of Omod Odol in 2013 became a great setback for the Anywaa fighters. The people who were put in jail with Ngeeli Oliru were Omod Okoth (Maiber), Paul Omod, Ojulu Gemechu, and many other people who were captured from the team of Omod Odol and the team of Obang Oluuch. There were seventeen Anywaa prisoners at the federal prison in total. In 2007, Bare Agid, Omod, and Kaunda Oman went to Eritrea and stayed with a group of forty-four other Anywaa militia members. However, Bare Agid was jailed in Eritrea and managed to escape to Uganda. While he was in a Uganda refugee camp, he was captured by the government of Uganda and handed over to the government of Ethiopia in 2015. Bare Agid stated:

> When I was in Eritrea, Okello Akway came, and I asked him to join my group since we were struggling for the same purpose. Okello Akway rejected my invitation. The next time I saw him was in the federal prison when I was brought from Uganda.[9]

When Dr. Abiy Ahmed came to power in 2018, all the Anywaa prisoners were released from prison.

---

9. Interview with Commander Bare Agid (August 30, 2022).

Jekap Omod on the left with Commander Ngeeli Oliru on the right. This picture of Commander Ngeeli Oliru was taken in Abwobo woreda on August 31, 2022. Commander Ngeeli Oliru was born and raised in a small village called Chienthoa in Jor woreda. At the age of 18, Ngeeli Oliru joined the National Defense Force of Ethiopia and served his country. He is one of the Ethiopian heroes who served their country and fought at the battle of Badme (Ethio-Eritrea war), guerilla wars against the TPLF government, Murle criminals, Nuer invaders, GLF, and the OLF/A-Shene. Ngeeli also fought in multiple wars against the TPLF government after the Anywaa genocide on December 13, 2003. Even though he spent most of his life in different wars, Ngeeli managed to have seven children with two different wives. Ngeeli has two sisters: Abang and Akello.

Chapter 12

The Anywaa People Post-Genocide

AFTER THE ANYWAA GENOCIDE on December 13, 2003, the Anywaa people faced unprecedented emigration to refugee camps located in Sudan, Kenya, and Uganda. Over thirty thousand Anywaa people left their ancestral lands and went into exile. Most of them are still in refugee camps, but some of them are currently living in the United States (the majority of them in Minnesota), Canada, Australia, England, and Europe. The first wave of massive emigration took place during the genocide. Then, the second largest emigration took place after the genocide because of oppression, jailings, beatings, land grabbing, forced villagization, and being labeled *"shifta,"* which means bandits. Due to the intense resistance by the Anywaa guerila fighters, Anywaa young men in Gambella faced tremendous atrocities committed by the government as they were suspected of either collaborating with the guerilla fighters or members.

In 2010, the federal government of Ethiopia came up with a villagization program for four main regions: Gambella, Benishangul-Gumuz, Somali, and Afar.[1] Historically, the Anywaa people lived along the major riverbanks in Gambella such as Openo, Alworo, Gilo, Akobo, Oboth, Dikony, and Agwenymals. They lived on these rivers where they cultivated the lands and passed it onto their kids throughout generations for centuries. They mainly grew maize and sorghum and depended on running water for drinking, cooking, washing, farming, and fishing. For the Anywaa people, land is a part of their identity. Within the Anywaa tribe, they divided

---

1. Horne, "Waiting Here for Death."

The Anywaa People Post-Genocide

themselves into subclans called *dhi-øtø*. Each *dhi-øtø* are known by the village in which they reside and lived in for generations. All the Anywaa lands, rivers, and forests have their own Anywaa owners, and they are called *week ngoomo* in Dha-Anywaa. *Week ngoomo* means the "owner of the lands" or the "fathers of the lands," and they have the duty to pray for the lands, rivers, and forests that belong to them. It is in the Anywaa tradition that before fishing, the owners of the land must pray to the river to prevent everyone from any harm, including snake bites or crocodile attacks. They do the same thing during the hunting season: the owners of the forests must pray to the land and forest so that the hunters get back home safely and nobody gets lost or injured. In the Anywaa lands, there are places and sacred forests that were worshiped and respected; you cannot cut down a tree in any of these forests or even crush a grass. The villagization program that was enforced on the Anywaa has ripped them off their social life, and it also led to abuses and violation of their human rights. This program displaced thousands of the Anywaa people from the fertile lands that they have depended on for generations.

On January 16, 2012, Human Rights Watch (HRW) published a report based on interviews they had with over one hundred residents that were affected by the forced villagization program that took place in Gambella in the year 2010. Based on their investigation, they concluded that the forced villagization program that took place in Gambella led to the relocation of the Anywaa people from the fertile lands they were cultivating for years to new villages with dry and poor quality lands; the relocated population faced hunger and starvation; students were forced to stayed out of school; women faced harassment, beatings, and rape by the government soldiers; and the Anywaa lands were then given to foreign and domestic investors.[2] Living under intimidation, beating, imprisonment, rape, and fear of the Ethiopian government forced the Anywaa people to leave their homeland and reside in refugee camps.

According to the Minister of Federal Affairs Shiferaw Teklemariam, the villagization program for Gambella was to "tackle poverty and ignorance" and to provide social services such as safe drinking water, good healthcare, education, access to market, road, power, and telecommunication.[3] The government of Ethiopia also referred to the villagization program as a "voluntary" program; however, the people were forcefully removed and

2. Horne, "Waiting Here for Death."
3. Horne, "Waiting Here for Death."

relocated. The relocated Anywaa people never had any access to clean water, good healthcare, education, or any good service that the Minister of Federal Affairs Shiferaw Teklemariam stated. Instead, their lands were leased to domestic and foreign investors. The main *woredas* that were affected by this program included Gambella, Abwobo, Dimma, Gog, Itang, Jor, and Godere. All these areas, apart from Godere, are inhabited by the Anywaa people while Godere is in the Majang zone. The poor Anywaa people in Gambella town were relocated to a place called *Wang-Carmie*. They were relocated because of the "master plan" that the government came up with. These were poor elderly and women who were living in traditional huts, and their lands were given to people with money to build better houses. None of them were compensated for their lands and destroyed houses. The only promise that was given to them was free grains from the government for the first six months and bigger lands for farming. One of the former residents from Gambella town stated:

> We were told this place should have this type of building, and so on and "you have not done that so we will relocate you to Carmie. You should have certain building standards, so we will allocate this land to the highlanders who will build to the standards contained in the master plan. You are not in the right area for this type of construction."[4]

The houses that belonged to the Anywaa people were targeted for destruction in the name of the "master plan" without giving them enough time to build huts in the *Wang-Carmie* where they were relocated. Thus, they were forced to live under trees as they built new huts for themselves in Wang-Carmie. Those who refused to leave had their houses destroyed, giving them no option but to become homeless or go to Carmie. When they got defensive, they were jailed, intimidated, or beaten by the government soldiers.

The Anywaa in Dimma *woreda* were relocated so that their lands would be leased to the gold mining industries. According to HRW, the people in Dimma were removed from their lands and relocated to a place about a twelve-hour walk away. The Anywaa people in Dimma were forced to relocate during the time of harvest. Thus, the crops were left in the fields to be burnt down by the government soldiers. But when they moved to the new areas, they were not given enough food, and they were left to starve

---

4. Human Rights Watch interview with a former resident of Gambella town. Dadaab, Kenya, June 18, 2011.

with their children. One person who was interviewed by Horne from Dimma *woreda* stated:

> People left their crops behind then tried to return. Those who refused to go had their houses burned down by soldiers. Crops were destroyed. In [the village], where there were many mangoes and some sugar cane, government soldiers burned 100 houses.[5]

Dimma *woreda* is one of the Anywaa woredas with fertile lands and reserved gold. The gold in Dimma woreda attracts many mining industries. The Anywaa people were removed from their farms and land in Dimma woreda to clear the lands for gold exploration. The Anywaa people have historically lived closer to Akobo River for hundreds of years. They depended on the Akobo River for drinking water, cooking, washing, farming, fishing, and many other things. When they were removed from their villages on the river, they were replaced by domestic and foreign mining investors. Mining sites were opened on the river where the mining machine released sewage water back into the river. All the waste from mining sites is dumped into the river causing water pollution. The Akobo River used to be one of the cleanest rivers in Anywaa land. People could see fish in the water with their naked eyes while standing at the bank of the river; that's how clear and clean the water of Akobo used to be. However, after increased gold exploration on the river, the water became muddy and polluted. The water became unsuitable for drinking anymore, and it had to be boiled and filtered to drink it. Due to the lack of another source for freshwater, the Anywaa people had no choice but to keep drinking from the Akobo River. The villagization program made it also hard for the Anywaa women to fetch water. They had to walk for hours to get water from the river, which resulted in many Anywaa women getting raped on their way and children getting abducted by the Murle criminals. Since people also depended on hunting for food, the increasing deforestation caused by the gold explorers had caused the population of animals to decrease, and the fish in Akobo River were impacted as well.

People had no power, and they were not allowed to say anything against the villagization program. Those who were suspected of being anti-villagization or those who refused to leave were beaten and jailed by the government. One of the eyewitnesses interviewed by Horne stated:

---

5. Horne, "Waiting Here for Death."

> My father was beaten for refusing to go along [to the new village] with some other elders. He said, "I was born here—my children were born here—I am too old to move so I will stay." He was beaten by the army with sticks and the butt of a gun. He had to be taken to hospital. He died because of the beating—he just became more and more weak. Two other villagers were taken to Dimma prison.[6]

These cruelties and abuses by the government forces had forced the Anywaa people to flee to Sudan, Kenya, and Uganda refugee camps in large numbers. Thus, the Anywaa population in Gambella substantially decreased. People who spoke out against the government were put in jail, and the young people would be suspected of being *shiftas* (bandits) without any evidence and brutally beaten until they started vomiting blood. After the beating, they usually ended up dying a few weeks or months later. Another young man told HRW this:

> When I went back to my old village to gather belongings I was told [by a soldier], "Why are you here? You are thieves." I was then beaten with sticks, and I still have chest pain. The day before this a friend was killed by soldiers. He was beaten with guns and sticks, was vomiting blood, and died before we could treat him. He was 19 [years old]. Anuaks were crying during the beating, but no one could intervene—there were many soldiers there—and we are scared of them.[7]

The same abuses were committed by the soldiers in places like Abwobo woreda, mainly in Okuna and Chobokir, Gog woreda, and Opagna. These woredas have fertile lands; the Anywaa people in these areas were removed so the lands would be leased to foreign and domestic investors.

One of the domestic investors was a Saudi business tycoon Mohammed Al Almoudi living in Ethiopia. He was given 10,000 hectares of farmland in Pokedi, along the Alworo river. The people of Pokedi who lived on Alworo River for centuries were forcefully removed from their traditional farms just for Al Almoudi to take over. The company of Al Almoudi intends to increase the farmland to five hundred thousand hectares. Many people were relocated to the Perbongo settlement area. The traditional huts and farms around Alworo River were cleared by the Saudi Star. With no food provided for the relocated people, the only source of food they had was

---

6. Horne, "Waiting Here for Death."

7. Human Rights Watch interview with a former Dimma resident. Dadaab, Kenya, June 19, 2011.

The Anywaa People Post-Genocide

wild honey, green leaves, and plants' roots. Their farms, maize, sorghum, wild fruits, forests, and fish were gone. One Anywaa elder was interviewed by Felix Horne about his twenty-five-year-old son, a father of two who died of starvation, and said:

> He was out to look for wild fruits because he and his family are so hungry.... He was out with two friends, and then just collapsed. He was carried back very weak to the village by his two friends. Some watered-down maize [the remains of quon] was given to him. He took a few sips, said he needed a nap, and never woke up.[8]

The people of Ilea village were also removed from their traditional farms, and the land was leased to India's Karuturi Global Ltd. The Anywaa maize, sorghum, and groundnut crops that were left in the farms were cleared out by the company without the consent of the Anywaa people. India's Karuturi Global was allocated one hundred thousand hectares of land, with the expectation to increase it to three hundred thousand hectares. They destroyed the shea trees which the Anywaa people used as a source of cooking oil and food for generations. In total, the government of Ethiopia leased over 32 percent of total land area for agriculture, which led to the displacement and emigration of over 70,000 local Anywaa people. This was a pure violation of Ethiopian and international law by Meles Zenawi and the TPLF government.

On December 24, 2011, the international community put more pressure on the TPLF led government because of the Human Rights Watch reports on the Anywaa genocide and the crimes against humanity committed against the Anywaa people. Then, Meles Zenawi sent a team from Addis Ababa to Gambella to evaluate President Omod Obang Olom and his leadership. There was a journalist named Alem Seget among the team. The meeting was held at Afegubaye Adarash in Gambella with Omod Obang and his cabinet. There were four points in the agenda that the people from Addis Ababa came with:

1. Meles Zenawi should be left out of the Anywaa genocide, and only Omod Obang should be blamed for it, since Okello Akway was in Norway and he couldn't be blamed for it.

---

8. Horne, "Waiting Here for Death."

2. Omod Obang should be the one responsible for the Anywaa genocide since he was the person who wrote the 762 names of educated Anywaa men.

3. Omod Obang Olom was the person who sold the Anywaa lands to the foreign and domestic investors.

4. Omod Obang was a corrupt person who stole 83 million *birr* and built the Geeba Hotel in Gambella.[9]

After hearing all these accusations, Omod Obang said at the meeting that if he goes to jail, Meles Zenawi should go to jail with him because he was the person who ordered him to write down the names of educated Anywaa men to be killed. Omod Obang Olom defended himself stating that he didn't kill a single person besides writing the names and sending them to the federal government. Okello Akway said:

> When Omod Obang said that, journalist Alemseget published it and the news went viral. I even saw that report from Norway. Those who were sent to Gambella to arrest him didn't succeed because he exposed what Meles Zenawi did.[10]

Omod Obang Olom[11] stayed in power until the death of Meles Zenawi on August 20, 2012. The news of Meles Zenawi's death came after he went missing for a few weeks prior to August 20. The cause of his death was kept secret by the TPLF members. Some people suggested that the surprising confrontation of journalist Abebe Gellaw might have played a role in accelerating the death of Meles Zenawi. The late prime minister was giving a speech about food security at the G8 Summit on May 18, 2012, when Abebe Gellaw started shouting:

> Meles Zenawi is a dictator! Meles Zenawi is a dictator! Free Eskinder Nega! Free political prisoners! You are a dictator. You are committing crimes against humanity. Food is nothing without freedom! Meles has committed crimes against humanity! We Need freedom! Freedom! Freedom!

In shock, Prime Minister Meles Zenawi bowed his head while Abebe was shouting. His chin dropped and he stared at the floor the whole time,

---

9. Interview with Okello Akway (August 29, 2022).

10. Interview with Okello Akway (August 29, 2022).

11. Omod Obang Olom (Okici) was the president of Gambella from September 29, 2005, to 2012. He was a member of the GPUDM.

ashamed of being exposed and embarrassed in front of the international community. Though the cause of his death was never revealed to the public, some people argued that the shock he had from Abebe Gellaw might have contributed to his death. When he died, Hailemariam Desalegn became his successor. When he became the prime minister, Hailemariam Desalegn brought Omod Obang to Addis Ababa and replaced him with Gatluak Tut Khot.

When he was in Europe, Omod Obang Olom was interviewed by the ESAT on March 22, 2017, about the Anywaa genocide, and he blamed the killing of the Anywaa people on TPLF officials and Meles Zenawi. During the interview Omod Obang stated that he was called by Meles Zenawi and was told that all the land in Gambella would be sold to investors since the population in the region is small compared to the land. According to him, the people who carried out the villagization program and the selling of the Anywaa land, which led to the displacement of thousands of Anywaa people from their ancestral land, were Abay Tsehay and Dr. Gebre-Aba Barnabas. Due to his involvement in the Anywaa genocide, Omod Obang was denied asylum both in Europe and United States of America. The only place that he was allowed in was the Philippines. When he was in the Philippines, Omod Obang was interviewed by the International Consortium of Investigative Journalists (ICIJ). During the interview, he confessed that the villagization program in Gambella was done using the money given to Ethiopia by the World Bank. Omod Obang told ICIJ:

> If we were not ordered by the federal government to reallocate the World Bank budget for the program [Villagization Program], the program would not be possible.[12]

Even though the World Bank denied the accusation by many organizations, their funds to Ethiopia played a bigger role in the villagization program which led to the suffering, rape, forced displacement, illegal detention, deaths, and many other human rights abuses on the Anywaa people. The World Bank was also responsible for the suffering of the Anywaa people during this villagization program because they chose to defend, turned a blind eye, and denied what was happening to the Anywaa people on the ground. Omod Obang Olom died in the Philippines in 2018, and his body was taken back to Gambella.

---

12. Chavkin, "New Evidence Ties World Bank."

Chapter 13

Living under the Oppression

ON JANUARY 19, 2012, Omod Obang Olom was removed from his position after admitting his involvement and the role that Meles Zenawi played in the Anywaa genocide in 2003. The federal government of Ethiopia appointed Gatluak Tut Khor to be the president of Gambella based on Omod Obang's recommendation. Under the leadership of Gatluak Tut Khor, the conflict between the Anywaa and Nuer became a day-to-day activity. This was another systematic and intentionally designed tactic to keep killing the Anywaa people and blaming it on tribal conflicts. While these conflicts were taking place, many TPLF members took out millions of *birrs* of loans from the Development Bank of Ethiopia (DBE) in the name of investment in Gambella. Many domestic investors in Gambella were the members of TPLF and Tigrayan ethnic group. Most of the lands that they took in the name of investment in Gambella were cleared and left without anything being done on them. The majority of those TPLF investors disappeared with the money they loaned from the Development Bank of Ethiopia and built hotels, houses, and business centers in Tigray instead. They never paid back the loans. Thus, the bank holds most of the land in the place of the loans taken from them even though those individuals who disappeared with the money didn't own the lands. Most Anywaa people also believe that the Development Bank of Ethiopia discriminated against the indigenous people of Gambella and intentionally denied them loans. Even people who satisfied all the requirements for securing loans. Most people who had access to loans from the DBE were from the Tigrayan ethnic group.

Living under the Oppression

In addition to the lack of opportunities and the denial of loans to start business or investment, illegal detention of the Anywaa youths became very common, especially when people got closer to the holidays such as Ethiopian New Year, Fasika, or any special regional celebration. Any Anywaa young man who is found walking at day or night without an ID would be taken to prison and labeled as a thief. Sometimes, when young people were sitting in a group playing games like chess, card games, or dominos, the police would suddenly arrive, chase after the youths, and take them to police stations until the holiday was over. Young men with dreadlocks, young men who were making money by picking onions, those who chew khat, and those who were just trying to enjoy their day by gambling, playing foosball, or pool were considered as troublemakers and thieves by the federal forces, and they were more likely to get arrested, beaten, or even shot if they tried to resist an arrest or tried to escape.

In 2016, one of the worst atrocities occurred under the leadership of Gatluak Tut which he got away with: youths were brutally murdered in the regional prison by the Nuer criminals and police. The conflict started when an Anywaa driver named Ajalara Ojulu[1] had a feud with Gatluak Buom Pal over a plot of land. As a vice dean administrator at Gambella Teachers and Health Science College, Gatluak Buom Pal tried to use his power to forcefully take the land of Ajalara Ojulu, and Ajalara decided to take the issue to court. That was when Gatluak Buom Pal took out the handgun he was carrying and shot Ajalara in one arm. Gatluak Buom never faced serious charges for attempted murder. That angered the Anywaa people in Gambella town, and the Anywaa youths started throwing rocks with the Nuer youths. The day before this conflict took place, many Anywaa youths were thrown into prison like the government under Gatluak Tut normally did until the holiday was over. Many youths in Gambella were thrown in jail by the local government in preparation for the tenth Ethiopian Nations, Nationalities and People's Day that was going to be celebrated on Wednesday December 9, 2015. The number of people in jail drastically increased,

---

1. Ajalara Ojulu was a driver for the vice president of Gambella region, Olero Opiew. When this incident took place, Gatluak Buom Pal was the vice dean for administration in the Gambella Teachers Education and Health Science College. After the election of 2021, he created a rebel organization and named it Gambella Liberation Front (GLF). Gatluak Buom was put in jail after shooting Ajalara Ojulu, but he was released quickly without any charges.

and even the food provided by Catholics in Gambella became insufficient for all the prisoners. Awinya Nyegilo[2] stated:

> Many youths were thrown in jail because of the Ethiopian Nations, Nationalities and People's Day that was hosted by Gambella. Whenever they find youths in the town, they would arrest them and bring them to jail. The jail became so crowded, while they were still bringing many youths to jail.[3]

On May 11, 2008, E.C. (or January 20, 2016), in the evening, there was a conflict that took place in college after Gatluak Buom was put in jail. The fighting started between Anywaa and Nuer individuals over food in the cafeteria which led to throwing rocks between the two ethnic groups on campus. This conflict grew and Nuer in Newland went on to attack the Anywaa neighbors around Tier-Jwieni and 04 kebele, burning down houses in the area. They were also using heavy weapons, and the ENDF and Federal police escorted them back to Newland without disarming or holding them accountable. This conflict split the special forces into two. The Nuer special forces supported their people, while the Anywaa special forces sided with the Anywaa people.

According to Awinya Nyegilo, the highlander security guards who were working in the jail started saying that the Nuer police were planning something about a potential attack against the Anywaa people in jail. On the same date, Wednesday January 20, 2016, the Nuer people in jail started making knives, steel with sharpened ends was turned into spears and all kinds of things that could be used as a weapon. When the Anywaa people saw that, they also started doing the same thing, preparing themselves in case of any possible attack. However, when the Nuer security guards saw that, they started taking all sharp materials from the Anywaa people but not the Nuers. During the night, Awinya stated:

> The Nuer security guards came to our room in the evening, and they wanted to relocate the Nuer people who were sleeping in our room. When the Anywaa people saw that, they refused that the

---

2. I interviewed Awinya Nyegilo Ojaay on October 2, 2023. He was born and raised in Anyaali village, one of the villages in Baat-Openo. He studied agriculture and graduated in 2015. Awinya Nyegilo was put in prison on August 29, 2015, with twelve other people in suspicion of the deaths of two people (a father and a son) in Pinymala. He stayed in jail for about five months without getting any justice. He was a survivor of the massacre of Anywaa youths in prison.

3. Interview with Awinya Nyegilo Ojaay (October 2, 2023).

Living under the Oppression

Nuer shouldn't be relocated. That night, we surely understood that something bad was going to happen to us. So, the Nuer prisoners were not relocated anywhere because we refused.[4]

On Thursday, January 21, 2016, there was no Anywaa security guard in the prison because they were told that only the Nuer and highlander security guards would be working that day. The excuse was to prevent any further conflict between the Anywaa special forces or police and the Nuer special forces or police. This was a plan to kill the Anywaa prisoners without any Anywaa security guard around. As a survivor and an eyewitness, Awinya Nyegilo Ojaay described the day of the Anywaa massacre in prison as follows:

> In the morning of Thursday Jan 21, 2016, we could see that the atmosphere in the prison was not good. There was an Anywaa elder named Akarekaa who came to Gambella from South Sudan and worked as a driver. He was jailed because he hit a *bajaj*[5] with the car while he was on duty. Akarekaa talked a lot with the highlander security guards, and they had a good relationship. In the morning, the highlander guards told him that things were not good, and he came and shared that with us. Akarekaa also told us that there was a bomb that was sneaked inside the prison. So, he warned us to be very careful and vigilant. I was sitting by the entrance at that time selling pasta for one Anywaa woman who was brought from Pinyudo. While I was sitting and selling pasta, there was an old Nuer man who pretended to be a pastor (pastors are allowed to visit inside the prison and preach or give messages to the prisoners) and he was meeting with the Nuer people in different small groups. He was going around like that, and I didn't know what he was meeting about. Then the bell rang, and it was time for money distribution.

The fight in the prison started during money distributions for the prisoners. Whenever it is time for the distributions, leaders from each building would go and take the money. Then, they would distribute them to their inmates who are staying in the same rooms. One Anywaa went and asked for his money from their leader who was Nuer. He wanted to have his money

---

4. Interview with Awinya Nyegilo Ojaay (October 2, 2023).

5. *Bajaj* is a three-wheeler mainly manufactured in India. It is used as a means of transportation in many cities of Ethiopia. Due to the lack of taxis in Gambella town, *bajajes* are used more often for transportation.

so he could buy a stew to eat with his *kwon*[6] *(quon)* that he had already prepared. The Nuer leader refused, stating that Anywaa people will not get their money that day. The Anywaa person thought that he was just joking, so he asked again calmly. But he was punched by the Nuer, and all the Nuer people stood up and started throwing rocks at all the Anywaa around. This took place around 9:00 a.m. When the Nuer started throwing rocks, some people were just in the shower, some were sleeping in the rooms, and some were beading. At this time, the number of Nuer security guards were unusually high in prison compared to the highlanders' guards, and there was no single Anywaa guard.

> When people started screaming and running around, the Nuer security guards fired more gunshots than I have ever heard before in my life. I told my mom, brother, and friends that I had never heard weapon sounds like that before. Whenever we tried to run from the Nuer who were armed with knives, sharp steel, sticks, and rocks, they would fire bullets at us to prevent us from running away. The Nuer security guards did that so that we could be killed by the Nuer prisoners with knives, sharp steel, and rocks instead of killing us by gunshots. I ran into a shop of a highlander, and one Nuer saw me. When he saw me, he threw a rock at me, and he missed my leg. That was when I climbed up the building and went on top of the roof. There was one Anywaa man who climbed up too, and his name is Okwom. We stayed up there watching the Anywaa prisoners getting chased and fired at by the security guards.
>
> When I was staying on the roof with Okwom, he told me that he wanted to jump down, and I warned him not to jump. But he didn't listen to me, so he jumped down. When he jumped, he was chased and beaten with firewood, and I was watching him. He kept running while his head was filled with blood, and all his clothes were red. He ran into the women's shower, and they stopped running after him. One Nuer saw me hiding on the roof, and he threw a long steel with a sharpened end at me. The steel missed me and hit the roof and pierced it. While the firing and killing was still going on, I decided to jump down so I could try to escape outside the prison. I jumped and ran toward the exit that's usually secured by the security guard. When I got there, I saw a Nuer security guard with a weapon, and he asked me where I was running. I told him that I wanted to get out. He told me that I was not going anywhere,

---

6. *Kwon:* a traditional Anywaa food made with corn flour. It can be eaten by dipping it in any kind of stew.

while lowering his weapon. So, I ran inside the women's shower and hid there. All of this happened around 9 a.m., and we reached 10 a.m. without any federal forces showing up, even though they were not very far from the prison. Eleven a.m. passed, 12 p.m. passed, and at around 1 p.m. the ENDF and Federal Police came to the prison.

We were hiding inside the shower at that time. While we were hiding inside there, I looked out through a small window and saw the Nuer who was carrying a bomb. I told the other Anywaa people in the room that we may not survive, because he could throw the bomb inside anytime. He noticed that we were hiding inside. I also saw a Nuer security guard hitting the butts of Akarekaa and Agwa Oganda who were already lying on the ground dead. When the federal forces arrived, they collected everyone, including us who were hiding in the shower. That was when we learned about the people who were killed. One of my cousins, who was sick, was killed. His name is Ocan Obuy. Akarekaa also was killed because he was one of the main targets. Agwa (Lwaal) Oganda was killed. Agwa Oganda and Akarekaa were killed together. They were brought out of the room and killed. There was also a young man named Mombasa Okach, he was killed while taking a shower. One police officer who was brought from Abwobo to Gambella prison was also killed. I don't remember his name. There was one young man from Nyikwo village who was killed, and I also don't remember his name either. Young man named Agaak from Ibaago village was among the killed people. There was one person that I don't remember his name. The total number of people who were killed reached eight people. One person who was left on the ground unconscious was taken to the hospital and survived.[7]

On the evening of Thursday, January 21, 2016, all the Anywaa people prisoners who survived were taken to Abwobo woreda prison, and they reached Abwobo prison at around 7 p.m. The bodies of the victims were taken to the Gambella regional hospital and laid down in one large plastic sheet for people to identify their relatives. The cruelty that was committed to them was indescribable: their faces were not recognized by their families, as their heads and faces were swollen and smashed during the beatings. Their eyes were gouged out. The people who were shot, their gun wounds were pierced so that they would not appear to be killed by the guards. The eyes of the victims were gouged out by a Nuer woman who was a police officer. Nobody was held accountable for this atrocity committed to the youths

7. Interview with Awinya Nyegilo Ojaay (October 2, 2023).

in prison, and their families never received justice. On Friday morning, January 22, 2016, Administrator of Anywaa Zone Othow Okoth (Ngoomagora) visited the prisoners who survived. This became the first time in Gambella in which people were brutally killed in prison with the support of the security guards. The federal forces could have intervened quickly, but they waited for hours before intervening, which led to the deaths of many youths; most of them were not criminals. For instance, Mombasa Okach was just one of the youths who were rounded up in prison because of Ethiopian Nations, Nationalities and People's Day. The Nuer people who were left in Gambella prison were released on Friday, including the ones who were involved in the killings. Nobody held them accountable. The Anywaa people in Abwobo did contribution for the prisoners who were taken to Abwobo Prison because all their clothes and belongings were looted in jail during the massacre. This was one of the events that took place under the leadership of Gatluak Tut, and he was never held accountable for it.

In 2018, Dr. Abiy Ahmed Ali became the prime minister of Ethiopia, and he was celebrated all over Ethiopia. In a short period of time, Dr. Abiy Ahmed brought substantial change to Ethiopia and to the entire Horn of Africa. He started by releasing thousands of political prisoners from jails, including many Anywaa fighters who were captured by the TPLF government. Dr. Abiy also appointed the very first gender-balanced cabinet in the history of the country. He was applauded by the international community when he officially brought twenty years of long-term conflict between Ethiopia and Eritrea to an end. The conflict between Ethiopia and Eritrea had caused so many lives from both sides. Dr. Abiy Ahmed also participated in the war of Badme when he was in the military. The peace between these two countries was highly welcomed by the people living in both countries, and many families who were separated for a long time were able to reconnect and reunite again for the very first time. Dr. Abiy also made an agreement with the opposition parties outside the countries and invited them to pursue a democratic and peaceful struggle. Many opposition parties in Eritrea returned to Ethiopia to pursue a peaceful struggle. When Dr. Abiy traveled to the United States, he met with the leaders of opposition parties in the States and talked about reconciliation. He went above and beyond, playing a big role in resolving conflicts between Kenya and Somalia, as well as Djibouti and Eritrea. The Prime Minister Dr. Abiy Ahmed then won a Nobel Prize for Peace in 2019 because of the tremendous change he brought to Ethiopia and its neighboring countries. However, the change that Dr. Abiy

Ahmed brought to Ethiopia at that time did not reach some regions. Gambella was one of the regions that never received any political change.

For instance, the Anywaa fighters who were released from the federal prison were still labeled *shifta* by the local officials and securities; freedom of speech was still being violated; and young people were put in prison for speaking out or posting something on social media complaining about the leadership and poor governance in Gambella. When I visited Gambella in 2018, the youths in Gambella were fed up with the nepotism, corruption, and lack of job opportunities under Gatluak Tut's leadership. There were youths who graduated from different universities, and they were looking for jobs for at least three or more years without getting one. Those with relatives in the government were hired right away after they graduated from the universities, and that frustrated many youths who didn't know anyone in the government. Those with money were also more likely to get a job after school through bribery. The Gambella region is one of the regions in Ethiopia that hosts refugees. It is the only region in Ethiopia where the number of refugees is larger than the entire population of the host communities. Yet, the jobs available at the NGOs in Gambella are mostly taken by people from other regions in Ethiopia, mostly from Addis Ababa. The number of local people working for the NGOs is very few, even though most of them meet all the criteria and requirements. People have to know someone in the organization or bribe their way through. This has caused anger and frustrations among Anywaa youths in Gambella who were facing the highest rate of unemployment. In August of 2018, the Anywaa youths in Gambella shared their concerns about the issues in Gambella town during a meeting with Dr. Magn Cham. I was in Gambella on vacation at that time, and I attended the meeting.

During the meeting, the youths raised questions about the lack of job opportunities, nepotism, and corruption in the NGOs and bribery in the local government. Dr. Magn Cham and Mr. Oray Opiew were the only elders at the meeting. When the former deputy president Senay Akwor was contacted to give answers to the questions raised by the youths, they sent the two commissioners in Gambella, Okony Okello and a Nuer person named Chwol Kun. Outside the compound that we were meeting in was surrounded by Gambella special forces and some federal forces. The youth were peacefully having a meeting about the issues that they were facing under the leadership of Gatluak Tut and Senay Akwor, and the government sent many well-armed forces instead. The local government was still using force and intimidation to silence people, just like when the TPLF was in power. That showed a lack of political change in Gambella. When the two commissioners entered the building that we were having a meeting in, the youths were just sitting and having a normal conversation. Mr. Chwol Kun said:

> What we are seeing here is different from what we were told. We were told that the Anywaa youths were mobilizing to create chaos in the city, and instead of sending forces alone to disperse you, we decided to come and see it ourselves. The meeting is very peaceful, and you have all the right to meet and discuss your issues with the government.

What Mr. Chwol said was appreciated by everyone at the meeting and he was applauded. However, when commissioner Okony Okello from the Anywaa tribe talked, he was telling us (the youth) that since our issues only concerned the Anywaa youths we should be meeting in Abwobo, the center of Anywaa zone. That instigated anger among the youths. One youth raised his hand and said:

> As we meet here today, Dr. Abiy Ahmed Ali, the PM of Ethiopia, is in the United States meeting with Ethiopians. President Trump didn't tell him to go and meet with his people in Ethiopia. Why can't we meet in our city?

That received a lot of applause from everyone at the meeting. Though young people didn't get to talk with the deputy president, Senay Akwor, the youths planned to meet again and select leaders to lead the movement. This was the beginning of the Dhaldiim movement.

PART 4

Chapter 14

Dhal-diim

THE WORD DHALDIIM CONSISTS of two words: *dhal* and *diim*. *Dhal* means defying or resisting and *diim* means Oppression. So, the word *dhaldiim* in English means "defying oppression." The word *dhaldiim* was first used during the Anya Nya I movement against the Arab government of Sudan. It is the name that was given to the first camp that was formed for the Anya Nya I movement in Pochala. I dedicate this part of the book to Dr. Magn Cham, who was the founder of the Dhaldiim movement in Gambella, Ethiopia.

When Dr. Magn went back to Gambella in 2017, he stayed in the region for nine months observing the political situation in the region. Then, political change took place in the country, and Dr. Abiy Ahmed became the prime minister of Ethiopia in 2018. The PM Dr. Abiy Ahmed brought many changes and political transformations, and he was supported throughout the country. With all the transformations and changes that he brought to Ethiopia, the change never reached Gambella. Dr. Magn Cham started questioning the leadership in Gambella after witnessing the lack of support for the changes that Dr. Abiy brought to Ethiopia. He stated:

> When I looked around, there were no signs or demonstrations in support of Dr. Abiy's change. So, I had an idea to mobilize the youths and work to make sure that the changes that the PM Dr. Abiy Ahmed brought to the country gets to Gambella.[1]

---

1. Interview with Dr. Magn Cham (September 25, 2023).

According to Dr. Magn, he thought about this in the month of July 17, 2018. Dr. Magn continued and said:

> When Dr. Abiy went to Eritrea to reconcile Ethiopia with Eritrea, the president of Gambella, Gatluak Tut, was in the United States for treatment. When he came back to Gambella, I thought that he would talk about how to bring change to Gambella during the meeting. However, he was talking about the changes and things that Dr. Abiy Ahmed had done in Ethiopia. I had a question why he was reporting about the things that we already knew. We were here in Ethiopia when Dr. Abiy Ahmed brought all these changes, but Gatluak Tut was in the United States. Why was he talking about the things that we already knew and not about what he was going to do in Gambella?[2]

When Dr. Magn Cham went to Addis Ababa and came back to Gambella, he was determined to bring political change to Gambella. He believed that a political transformation was needed in Gambella, and that the regional leadership should be changed. Dr. Magn Cham reached out to a young leader named Mesael Ojulu Okongo and asked how he could meet the youths in Gambella. He said:

> I reached out to Mesael through Facebook Messenger because I knew that he was an influential young man in Gambella. He was a lecturer at Gambella University.[3]

This was how Dr. Magn Cham heard about the meeting organized by the Anywaa Students Association for Development for students from first to ten grades in Gambella. During this meeting on July 24, 2018, Dr. Magn was welcomed as a distinguished guest even though he showed up without prior notice. He was also invited to help hand out awards to the students who finished school as top three ranks in their classes. After the end of the program, Dr. Magn said:

> I expressed my gratitude for welcoming me to the program, and I told them that I was there to meet the youths. So, I shared my ideas with them about the changes that we needed to bring to Gambella. I told them that if they don't stand up for themselves, there will be no change in Gambella. I also let them know that young people are the ones who bring a revolution and change.[4]

2. Interview with Dr. Magn Cham (September 25, 2023).
3. Interview with Dr. Magn Cham (September 25, 2023).
4. Interview with Dr. Magn Cham (September 25, 2023).

The youth leaders who led the meeting were Didumo Obang (Nyaang Gaala), Omod Opodhi, and Cham Ochudho. Those were the leaders of the Anywaa Students Association for Development in 2018. After hearing about the ideas that Dr. Magn shared with them, the leaders of the Anywaa Students Association for Development planned to have another meeting where more youths were invited.

On July 28, 2018, the next meeting was held, and many youths were present at the meeting. Dr. Magn Cham called Obang Oguta, Oray Opiew, Omod Obol, and Omod Ochala and shared with them the meeting he arranged with the youths. Obang Oguta, Oray Opiew, and Dr. Magn attended the meeting. During the meeting, Dr. Magn said:

> I told the youths that we needed to start a movement to change the regional leadership. We needed new young leaders in the Gambella region.[5]

Young people supported Dr. Magn's ideas, and they all expressed their ideas as well. The Anywaa youths wanted transformation in Gambella due to the lack of job opportunities, mismanagement of natural resources in Gambella, land grabbing by foreign and domestic investors, and refugee crisis in the Gambella region. Young people also wanted the Itang Special District to be changed back to Itang District, and they wanted Gambella town to be led by someone from Gambella town. Dr. Magn didn't have a hard time convincing the youths. They all wanted change in Gambella, and the only thing that they lacked was having someone to initiate a movement. That was done by Dr. Magn, and the movement started. During the meeting, they appointed five mobilizing committees. The mobilizing committees were Obang Oguta, Didumo Obang, Obang Kiru, Cham Ochudho, and Pen Ojulu. The first chairman of the movement was Obang Oguta, Didumo Obang (Nyaang Gaala) was the vice chairman, Obang Kiru was the secretary, Cham Ochudho was the mobilizing and information person, and Pen Ojulu was chosen to be a member, but he refused. Dr. Magn Cham then became an advisor for the committees. According to Dr. Magn, the goal of the movement was to change how politics was played in the Gambella region.

When the elected committees started their work, the regional government started noticing it, and the regional leadership began interfering to stop the movement. According to Dr. Magn, the vice president of Gambella, Senay Akwor, tried to stop the movement but he failed. Many young

---

5. Interview with Dr. Magn Cham (September 25, 2023).

people joined the movement, and it became too strong. At that time, there was a Facebook page called "Deeloneen Pergambella," and it was already exposing the injustices in Gambella. Whenever there was a meeting among the youths, Deeloneen Pergambella would post about the meeting, referring to the group as "Dhaldiim." On August 16, 2018, the youth group had a meeting that was attended by Vice President Senay Akwor, Okony Buya, and Oguula Ojulu (who was the administrator of Anywaa zone), Pastor Omo Okwori, and Pastor Peter Agwa Ochala. Dr. Magn Cham stated:

> Since Deeloneen Pergambella had been posting and referring to the movement as Dhaldiim, Senay Akwor opened the meeting by asking "are you not Dhaldiim?" And young people in the hall responded "yes, we are!" Followed by loud applause from the youths.[6]

The name of the movement then became Dhaldiim after the meeting. During that meeting, the points that were raised by the young people included addressing corruption in Gambella, freedom of speech and real democracy in Gambella, addressing the unfair distribution of lands to foreign and domestic investors without including the local communities, the Itang woreda shouldn't be a special woreda, NGOs and ARRA in Gambella were not giving jobs to the local youths, and the question of why the refugees are staying in Anywaa zone only.

One of the things that Dhaldiim did, which brought panic to the regional leadership, was the great welcoming of the human rights activist Obang Metho to Gambella. Due to the changes that Dr. Abiy Ahmed brought to Ethiopia, the opposition's political leaders, activists, and journalists who were not allowed to come to Ethiopia during the TPLF governments were welcomed back to Ethiopia. They were highly welcomed by their supporters throughout Ethiopia. Activist Obang Metho, a human rights activist, went back to Ethiopia. When Obang Medho went to Gambella on September 17, 2018, the Dhaldiim youths warmly received him from Gambella Airport and escorted him throughout the town. Young people from Pignudo, Abwobo, Dimma, Gambella town, Abol, and many areas in the Gambella region came together in big numbers and received Mr. Obang Medho. According to Dr. Magn, Mr. Obang Medho was welcomed in a great turnout that had never happened in Gambella town before. After

---

6. Interview with Dr. Magn Cham (September 25, 2023).

welcoming Obang Medho, there was a meeting the next day and Dr. Magn restated the goals of Dhaldiim during the meeting.

The growth of the Dhaldiim movement had caused panic not only to the local government officials but to the Nuer community as well. On September 23, 2018, the president of Gambella, Gatluak Tut, imprisoned some Nuer youths. According to Dr. Magn, those Nuer youths were put in prison for no legitimate reason. Thus, the Dhaldiim leaders went to Gambella prison and demanded the release of the Nuer youths who were jailed by Gatluak Tut. One of the Nuer youths that was released that day became known by his new nickname: Ruach Dhaldiim. Dr. Magn said:

> After we released Ruach Dhaldiim from Gambella prison, we went to the Police Commission to check if there were Nuer youths illegally detained over there. When we arrived at the Police Commission, the Nuer police who were there got their weapons ready. We asked them to release any Nuer youths who were illegally detained. But they denied that nobody was detained there illegally.[7]

When the federal police heard about this, they tried to calm the situation by dispersing the crowded youths. *Shaleqa*[8] Terefe told the crowd that there were no detained youths and asked everyone to leave and go home. Dr. Magn continued and said:

> When we got by my house, we had a little meeting with the youths and told them to meet me the next day morning [September 24, 2018] by my house so we can go to Mikir Beth and demand those leaders [President Gatluak Tut and Vice President Senay Akwor] to step down from their positions.[9]

After the youths left, the ENDF arrived in Gambella town and headed to Dr. Magn's house. They surrounded Dr. Magn's house in large numbers with all kinds of weapons. Dr. Magn said:

> They were carrying all kinds of heavy weapons. I think the only weapon they didn't bring was a tank![10]

After he was informed by his brother James, Dr. Magn went out of his room and saw the top leaders of ENDF inside his compound, but the rest of the

---

7. Interview with Dr. Magn Cham (September 25, 2023).
8. *Shaleqa* is the Amharic word for "commander of a thousand."
9. Interview with Dr. Magn Cham (September 25, 2023).
10. Interview with Dr. Magn Cham (September 25, 2023).

forces were outside surrounding the compound. When the Anywaa people saw the ENDF surrounding Dr. Magn's house, they also crowded in the area standing to see what was going to happen. This created a big tension between the ENDF and the Anywaa people standing outside Dr. Magn's house. The colonel of the ENDF in Gambella, Colonel Woldu, and his personal guards were looking for Dr. Magn Cham in his house. Even though they didn't have a warrant, they illegally entered Dr. Magn's house by force. Dr. Magn said:

> When they said that they were looking for me, I invited them and gave them seats to sit down. Then, they asked me if I was the leader of Dhaldiim. I told them that I was not the leader of Dhaldiim. When they asked who the leader was, I told them that Dhaldiim was led by the youths, not me. I also told them to ask the youths, and that they will tell them who the leaders of Dhaldiim were. They wanted to take me, but the tension outside my house between the ENDF and the Anywaa people was not good. The Anywaa people had nothing in their hands, but they were all ready and standing facing the soldiers. So, the ENDF leaders were scared that if they took me with them, something bad would happen. The only thing that Colonel Woldu did was take a picture of me with his phone without my permission and he left with his soldiers.[11]

During the night, a young man named Okello Ojwato was killed by the Nuer people, which shifted all the things to be between Anywaa and Nuer. Even though Dhaldiim movement was to challenge the regional leadership, the Nuers in leadership saw Dhaldiim as a movement against the Nuer people because the president was Nuer by ethnicity. So, they mobilized their youths to defend the leadership in Gambella through violence and killed Okello on the night of September 23, 2018. The Dhaldiim movement was not specifically targeting the Nuer leaders alone, but the entire regional leadership. According to Dr. Magn Cham, this movement was to bring Dr. Abiy's change to Gambella, and it has nothing to do with the Nuer officials. That was why they released the Nuer youths who were illegally detained by president Gatluak Tut.

On September 24, 2018, in the morning, the youths went to Dr. Magn's house as planned. The youths were exasperated and devastated by Okello's death, and they wanted to take revenge. However, they were advised by Dr. Magn to go and bury Okello instead. While Dr. Magn and some youths

---

11. Interview with Dr. Magn Cham (September 25, 2023).

were at the burial ceremony of Okello, some Nuers went to Omiininga and created another conflict with the Anywaa people in the area. When the youths at the burial ceremony heard about that, they all rushed to Omiininga. Dr. Magn said:

> All the youths rushed to Omiininga to face the Nuers. When I tried to go with the youths, Chief (Kwaaro) Okwom Ojwato Okok[12] told me to not go. He stated that since I am the person who came up with the vision, I should not risk my life by going to such places because I will be the main target. This was the day that Kwaaro Okwom Ojwato Okok joined the Dhaldiim movement. Kwaaro Okwom also provided me with a safer room at his hotel since my home became a target of the government forces.[13]

Chief Okwom Ojwato Okok then went to Omiininga with the youths. When the youths reached Omiininga, the ENDF were already there, and they stood between the Nuers and the Anywaa youths. When the Anywaa youths were not able to reach the Nuers, they went back to downtown Gambella and searched for Nuer people who were caught up in the city. When they found one Nuer, they threw him off a high story building. The youths in the Baro-Mado area also burned tires on the streets because they were furious about the death of Okello. That was when the ENDF opened fire at youths and killed four children on September 24, 2018. According to Dr. Magn Cham, General Brehanu Telaun came to Gambella from Addis Ababa when things intensified. At the meeting on September 27, 2018, the Dhaldiim leaders expressed that they would go ahead and protest. However, General Brehanu Telaun stated that Dhaldiim should postpone the demonstrations to October 1 due to the curfew. He offered to provide forces to protect the people during the demonstrations and to prevent any violence.

On October 1, 2018, Dhaldiim held a big peaceful demonstration in Gambella town demanding the removal of the local leaders. This demonstration was the biggest demonstration ever carried out in the history of Gambella. Thousands of youths from different woredas in Gambella went to Gambella town for the demonstration. Almost all youths from different ethnic groups in Gambella joined the protest except the Nuer youths since the president was Nuer. The demonstration was carried out peacefully, and the demands of Dhaldiim written on a paper were presented to

---

12. Chief (Kwaaro) Okwom Ojwato Okok was the official chief of Pokedi.
13. Interview with Dr. Magn Cham (September 25, 2023).

local leaders. Omod Ochala read the letter, and the demonstration finished peacefully. The shopkeepers in Gambella town closed their shops out of fear of any possible conflicts. But the demonstration finished peacefully, and Dr. Magn and some Dhaldiim leaders went to the shopkeepers and asked them to open their shops and continue with their usual businesses. He said:

> We told them to not be afraid because we were peacefully protesting the bad leadership in Gambella, and it has nothing to do with the businesspeople. We told them that nobody would rob their property. So, they opened their shops and the usual businesses continued.[14]

On October 2 in the morning, the youths had a meeting with General Brehanu Telaun and Vice President Senay Akwor. According to Dr. Magn, about five thousand youths attended the meeting. But, when General Brehanu Telaun was speaking, he was siding with the local leadership. Dr. Magn said:

> When General Berhanu Telaun spoke, he was speaking with power and threats telling the youths that if they wanted, they could go to the forest and revolt just like they [TPLF] did. The youths were very angry because of his conversation. One of the youths responded and said, "Why are you threatening us? Don't you know our history? We are Anywaa and this is our land, you can't threaten us here. We will die here!"[15]

When he continued threatening, the youths stood up and started leaving the meeting. When the youths began leaving, General Brehanu Telaun started calling for Dr. Magn to bring back the youths to the meeting. After the meeting, Brehanu Telaun told Dhaldiim leaders to have another meeting again in the evening with General Mohammed Tessema, who would be coming to Gambella that evening. General Mohammed Tessema arrived in Gambella, and they arranged a meeting with the Dhaldiim leaders at 4 p.m. (10 p.m. local time). Dr. Magn Cham, Chief Okwom, and Dhaldiim leaders went to the meeting with General Mohammed Tessema, General Beheranu Telahun, President Gatluak Tut, Vice President Senay Akwor, and the security of Gambella.

---

14. Interview with Dr. Magn Cham (September 25, 2023).
15. Interview with Dr. Magn Cham (September 25, 2023).

DHAL-DIIM

During the meeting, Dhaldiim leaders made it clear that they wanted change in Gambella. Dr. Magn said:

> We told them that to have Dr. Abiy's change in Gambella, the leadership in Gambella must be replaced by young people with fresh minds. All the leaders who had been in leadership for over twenty-seven years need to be replaced. Everyone spoke during the meeting. General Mohammed Tessema also spoke very well.[16]

The Dhaldiim leaders also stated that the members of ENDF who killed four children on September 24, 2018, should be brought to justice. Furthermore, they demanded Gatluak Tut and Senay Akwor to step down from their positions. According to Dr. Magn, this was the day that Gatluak Tut and Senay Akwor understood that they were not the leaders of Gambella anymore. On October 3, General Mohammed Tessema called another meeting with the Dhaldiim leaders at 5 p.m. at the Grand Hotel. When Dhaldiim leaders and their advisors arrived at the hotel, he delayed the meeting by one hour to take a nap. So, the Dhaldiim leaders left and never went back. On October 4 in the morning, Dr. Magn Cham missed two calls from General Mohammed Tessema and Colonel Woldu. At this time Colonel Woldu had a good relationship with Dr. Magn Cham already. They didn't have a good relationship in the beginning because Colonel Woldu was told that Dr. Magn Cham was coming back to Gambella to take revenge for the Anywaa people who were killed on December 13, 2003. But he realized that Dr. Magn just wanted to have Dr. Abiy's change in Gambella and that he had no intention of taking revenge. Thus, they became good friends after the peaceful demonstrations and all the meetings with the generals. Dr. Magn Cham missed their calls, and he didn't return their calls. According to Dr. Magn, Colonel Woldu might have called him to let him know that he would be put in prison.

On October 4, Dr. Magn Cham, Chief Okwom, and the president of Dhaldiim Obang Oguta were detained and put in prison. According to Dr. Magn, the reasons that General Brehanu Telahum stated for their detentions were that the youths boycotted the meeting with him while Dr. Magn was present, that Dr. Magn spoke "harsh words" against him at the meeting, that Dr. Magn was accused of discrimination, and that since the four children who were killed by the federal forces were part of Dhaldiim, the Dhaldiim leaders should share responsibility. They were jailed for one month and five days and released on November 9. Dr. Magn said:

---

16. Interview with Dr. Magn Cham (September 25, 2023).

> We were released from the jail because they couldn't find any legitimate reason to keep us jailed. Judge Nyigwo released us, even though the Nuer judge above him didn't want us to be released.[17]

While they were in prison, Gatluak Tut and Senay Akwor were removed from their positions, and Omod Ojulu Obub and Thankuey Joack were appointed as the president and vice president of Gambella respectively. Dr. Magn stated:

> When Omod Ojulu Obub started working, the youths complained that they didn't want him because he was part of the TPLF led government for the last twenty-seven years. Since Dhaldiim is against the bad leadership under TPLF, Omod Ojulu Obub should not be the president because he was a part of that group. I advised them during the meeting and told them that we can try to work with Omod and try to correct him. If we stand against the new leadership, even the PM, Dr. Abiy would wonder about what the Gambella youths really wanted because the change of leadership was our goal. Many youths were not happy with my remarks, and even the Deeloneen Facebook page started writing negative things about me, like that I extinguished the fire of Dhaldiim. I was looking at the bigger picture: if we remove Omod Ojulu Obub, we may get another, worse president.[18]

After this meeting, Dhaldiim started to slow down and became less active because of Dr. Magn's suggestion to work with the new president Omod Ojulu Obub. According to Dr. Magn, Dhaldiim became weak because of him. However, the local government also played a role by recruiting the youths who were the main players and the backbone of the movement, such as Omod Samuel, Obang Oguta, Pen Ojulu, and a few others.

The new Dhaldiim leaders were elected on September 30, 2019. The new chairperson was Ojulu Ojulu, also known as Okunyi; Abang Kumudan, vice chairperson; Omod Opodhi, secretary; Ochan Ojho, communication director; Gabriel Wube, finance director; and Omod Obang, gender director. After functioning for a short time under pressure from the local government, Dhaldiim became dysfunctional. Young people started to be jailed by the government in the name of anonymous Facebook accounts. People who were targeted and accused of running these Facebook accounts were Ojho Ojulu, the chairperson of Dhaldiim Ojulu Ojulu, Ogala

---

17. Interview with Dr. Magn Cham (September 25, 2023).
18. Interview with Dr. Magn Cham (September 25, 2023).

Dhal-diim

Omod Cham, Abajedo Aganya, and Kalayeha Lamma Ogut. Ojulu Ojulu, Ogala Omod, and Abajedo Aganya were jailed. But Ojho Ojulu and Kalayeha Lamma Ogut were forced to leave Gambella town. The Dhaldiim movement then slowly stopped functioning as many youths were recruited by the local government. Some of them were organized in small groups (*maiber*[19]) and participated in the local businesses as *maibers*. Other youths were given jobs in government positions.

One of the main goals of Dhaldiim when it was founded by Dr. Magn Cham was to change the leadership in the Gambella region. Secondly, it was created to challenge the unfair hiring by the NGOs in Gambella region. According to Dr. Magn, there are about sixty-nine NGOs in Gambella and none of their employees were Anywaa or Nuer youths. But there were 409 registered youths from both Anywaa and Nuer communities who had bachelor's degrees but had no jobs. So, Dhaldiim was created to resolve this unemployment and lack of inclusiveness of the local communities to work in the NGOs in Gambella. Their main goal was to have the NGOs hire at least 50 percent of the workers from the local communities. Thirdly, the goal of Dhaldiim was to bring back the Itang Special District to Itang District. Itang should not be a special district since it belongs to the Anywaa zone, and it is one of the Anywaa's districts in Gambella. Fourthly, Dhaldiim wants Gambella town to be led by the Anywaa people since it is Anywaa land and belongs to the Anywaa people. Lastly, Dhaldiim wanted the refugees to be controlled and monitored by the government. The refugees should stay in their camps and stop getting involved in local political and social affairs. According to Dr. Magn, the only goal that Dhaldiim achieved was to bring change to the leadership in Gambella.

---

19. *Maiber* is the Amharic word for "association."

I interviewed Dr. Magn Ochala Cham (PhD) on September 25, 2023. This is a short introduction of who he is: Dr. Magn was born in Pinyudo, and he attended first grade in the area. Then, he moved to Abwobo and continued his education in second grade. When he finished second grade in Abwobo, Dr. Magn went back to Pinyudo for his third grade. He then moved to Gambella town where he continued his schooling from fourth to eighth grade. Dr. Magn attended high school in Addis Ababa (ninth to twelfth grade). When the Derg government was overthrown, Dr. Magn Cham went to Kenya as a refugee for about one year. After getting an asylum opportunity in the United States, he attended the University of Minnesota and got his bachelor's degree. He also got his master's and PhD in the United States. Dr. Magn has three children in the United States and two children in Gambella (during the time of the interview). After working in the United States, Dr. Magn went back to his homeland in Gambella in 2017 and became an investor.

Dhal-diim

The biggest demonstration that was held by Dhaldiim on October 1, 2018, which led to the removal of Gatluak Tut and Senay Akwor from their positions.

The welcoming of Obang Metho on September 17, 2018.

The biggest demonstration that was held by Dhaldiim on October 1, 2018, which led to the removal of Gatluak Tut and Senay Akwor from their positions.

Chapter 15

Lwaa-Ceri

THE ANYWAA PRISONERS WHO were kept in prison by the TPLF government were released when Prime Minister Dr. Abiy Ahmed Ali came to power in 2018. Most of them went back to Gambella where they were highly welcomed by the Anywaa people. Furthermore, the Anywaa militias (mostly GPLM members) who were staying in Eritrea also accepted the invitation of Dr. Abiy Ahmed to come back to Ethiopia and pursue a peaceful struggle. When they returned to Gambella, they faced criticism and unwelcome treatment from the people in the regional government. They continued to be labeled by the local officials as *shifta* which means "terrorists," despite the change and reconciliation that Dr. Abiy Ahmed came with. Ngeeli Oliru said:

> We told them [regional government officials] that we were not terrorists, but we were taking revenge for their brothers and sisters who were massacred by the government of Ethiopia.[1]

Most of the people who returned home were purposefully denied jobs in Gambella town. For instance, Commander Ngeeli Oliru was denied joining the militia in Gambella town. He stated:

> Senay Akwor and Gatluak Tut said that I am a killer who killed the Nuer and Gaale [highlanders]. So, they denied me any job in

---

1. Interview with Commander Ngeeli Oliru (August 31, 2022).

Gambella town and sent me to Jor woreda where I was appointed as the head of Jor militia.[2]

Ngeeli Oliru served in his position from 2011 E.C (2019) to 2013 E.C. (2021) in Jor woreda. Before Ngeeli Oliru was appointed in Jor woreda, Murle used to frequently attack the area and kidnap children, kill civilians, and steal cattle. After Ngeeli took over security in the area, he managed to stop the crimes that the Murle people used to commit on civilians in Jor. He restored peace in the area where women were able to freely collect cooking wood, children started moving from place to place without getting kidnapped, men started to hunt again without any fear, and the frequent attacks by the Murle criminals totally ceased. The three years that Ngeeli was in the local militia leadership were peaceful, and the people of Jor enjoyed their freedom of movement in the area and around. Few of those who were released from federal prison by Dr. Abiy joined the regional special forces, while many of them stayed without any job. Bare Agid, who had military experience, was given a job as the events recorder. When someone is getting married in Gambella town, or if someone gives birth to a new baby, Bare Agid would record that. This is something he had no background or experience in; he is a soldier. People like the former president of Gambella, Okello Akway, stayed jobless in Gambella.

As the general election of 2021 approached, all the registered political parties in Gambella started mobilizing their bases. The campaigning took place in Gambella town, and throughout the Anywaa zone, Nuer zone, and Majang zone. This election was well anticipated by the people since it was expected to be fair by many. As expected, the Prosperity Party in Gambella faced a great challenge from the Gambella People's Liberation Movement (GPLM) and Ethiopian Citizens for Social Justice Party (EZEMA).[3] Though it was apparent that the ruling party (PP) was using its power to deny the opposition parties to meet with their supporters at the government's halls, there was still hope for a fair election. That hope totally faded away during the day of election because it was rigged by the ruling Prosperity Party. For instance, the election in Jor woreda was rigged by the PP officials. Even

2. Interview with Commander Ngeeli Oliru (August 31, 2022).

3. GPLM and EZEMA were the popular parties in the Anywaa zone. GPLM was led by Peter Aman, while EZEMA was led by Dr. Omod Agwa. The Gambella Peoples for Peace and Justice Democratic Movement was led by Gatluak Buom. Unlike GPLM and EZEMA, the Gambella Peoples for Peace and Justice Democratic Movement was not popular and didn't get a voice in the region.

though GPLM was clearly leading in the beginning of the polling, the results drastically changed in favor of PP, which had fewer supporters in Jor woreda. The leaders of the militia were tried to be bribed by the local administrator named Okello Ocwor. Ngeeli Oliru stated:

> We were called into the office by the administrator of Jor woreda, Okello Ocwor. The people that I worked with were Gale Deng, Ocan Wa-apay, and Obang Odong. When four of us were called by Okello Ocwor, he handed me 34,000 *birrs* so that I could help them steal the election from the GPLM. I refused to take the money, and I told him that I sacrificed my life and fought for the people of Jor. So, I would never betray my people for 34,000 *birrs*. When I refused to take the money, the other three people with me also refused to take the money given to them and we left the office.[4]

The refusal to cooperate with the Prosperity Party in Jor woreda led to conflict between the PP officials and the leaders of the local militia. According to Ngeeli Oliru, the federal forces were hired by Okello Ocwor to arrest Ngeeli and his team, accusing them of siding with the GPLM Party even though they should be neutral. Ngeeli and his team refused to be arrested, and they picked up their weapons to fight back. Their willingness to fight those who were sent to arrest them scared the forces that were sent, and they decided to peacefully resolve the issue without taking them to prison. When the results of Jor woreda were announced, the Prosperity Party was announced as the winner. Among the 156 seats in the Gambella regional council, 149 seats were won by the ruling party (PP) and only 7 seats were won by the GPLM Party. The EZEMA Party won zero seats in the Gambella regional council. The election was delayed in some parts of the region including Gambella town because there were not enough ballots in some polling areas. This led to delays of counting and publicizing the results which made many people question the legitimacy of the election. The election was also rigged in Gog woreda.

The Creation of Lwaa-Ceri

Lwaa ceri contains two Anywaa words: *lwaak* and *ceri*. *Lwaak* means a clan or group, and *ceri* means honey badger. *Lwaa ceri* means a clan or group of honey badgers. A honey badger is a small animal that can be found in Africa, Asia, and the Indian subcontinent. It has very sharp teeth and

---

4. Interview with Commander Ngeeli Oliru (August 31, 2022).

powerful claws. The honey badger feeds on honey larvae, honey, rodents, and invertebrates such as arthropods. It is known for its fearlessness and courage. Despite its small size, a honey badger can fight a herd of lions if it feels threatened or attacked. Lwaa Ceri was the name of a group of Anywaa youths who followed in the footsteps of an American Anywaa named Chol Okey Opiew, who was killed on November 24th, 2021. The name Lwaa Ceri was created and given to the group by the king of Adongo in the year 2022, but the group was created by Chol Okey Opiew prior to 2022.

Chol Okey Opiew was a resident of Austin, Minnesota. He was a very active and loving person in the Austin community. Chol was a part of Amnesty International at Riverland Community College. In 2006, he became the first chairperson for the SPLM for the Austin chapter. In an interview done by Rocky Hulne for the *Austin Daily Herald*, Chol's son Ochan Okey stated:

> My father is the type of man who puts other people before himself. My dad is also a very hard worker and an amazing father. Providing for six children on his own, getting his degree, and working multiple jobs is not easy. Even through tough times, he persisted and pushed forward with a bright smile on his face.[5]

Chol was born and grew up in Akobo, South Sudan. At the age of 20, Chol Okey Opiew immigrated from Ethiopia to the United States, where he started a new life for himself. He kept fighting and advocating for the rights of South Sudanese until they received their independence in 2011. Chol raised his six children by himself while also helping new immigrants and refugees when they arrived in Austin and getting involved in Anywaa community activities. In 2021, Chol Okey Opiew traveled to Ethiopia to visit his family and homeland, Chiro. Chiro is the land of Anywaa people located in South Sudan. The Nuer people have occupied this Anywaa land in the last few years, forcing the people of Chiro to leave their ancestral lands and flee to other Anywaa villages around, and some relocated to refugee camps in Pinyudo in Ethiopia.

Chol Okey Opiew had a vision of returning his people to their ancestral land, Chiro. During my interview with Ngeeli Oliru, he stated that Chol Okey Opiew and fourteen other Anywaa men from Chiro land came from the South Sudan side and crossed into Ethiopia in 2021. At that time, Ngeeli was the head of the special forces in Jor woreda. As a head of the

---

5. Hulne, *Leaving a Mark*.

special forces, he received the information from South Sudan officials that a group of Anywaa men were heading to Ethiopia through Jor woreda, and their intention was to open an attack on Ethiopia. Ngeeli Oliru said:

> When I received the information, I looked for a way to meet them, and I contacted them. They told me that they were going to a village called Alaalli, they had no intention of opening any attack in Ethiopia. Their goal was to go and reclaim Chiro, which was forcefully taken by the Nuer invaders. They also wanted to move the Anywaa of Chiro in Gambella refugee camp back to their ancestral land in Chiro. The people in the leadership in the Gambella regional government were not happy about that.[6]

Ngeeli Oliru sent special forces to meet with Chol's team, and they were taken to King Wara-Joori of Yemiila. The special forces were led by a Nuer man named Luut. According to Ngeeli, they kept communicating with one another as they stayed with the king, and the security of Gambella was aware of his stay in Ethiopia. Chol and his team had a satellite phone which they used to communicate with Ngeeli Oliru and people from the United States like Dwel Jang and a person named Thatha. Those are the people of Chiro who wanted to restore Chiro and bring their people back to their land. The group also contained Anywaae from all over the places who wanted to help their brothers achieve this goal. Ngeeli Oliru said:

> Since what they were doing was for the Anywaa people to go back to their land, I went to Obang Kut and told him about Chol's team and what they wanted to do. Obang Kut was agitated and stated that we may get in trouble and even go to jail because the Nuer would not allow the Anywaa people to go back and reclaim their lands peacefully. I told Obang that we will not go to jail, if the regional government is not happy for the Anywaa to get back to their land and try to jail us for supporting this plan, then we will fight. We have been put in jail for more than enough! Obang was not convinced.[7]

On November 24, 2021, while Chol Okey Opiew was in Pinyudo with his relatives, he was stabbed in the stomach twice and shot by Nyikanga Makwach Adhom. Chol was rushed to the hospital where he passed away. Nyikanga was a close relative to Chol, and he was helped and taken care of by Chol Okey Opiew as a family. After killing Chol, Nyikanga was taken

6. Interview with Commander Ngeeli Oliru (August 31, 2022).
7. Interview with Commander Ngeeli Oliru (August 31, 2022).

into custody. Chol Okey Opiew was the person who formed this group to reclaim the land of Chiro along with Ojulu Ajak, Obang Maak, and Weny-naam Okony. Those three people did not stop after the death of Chol Okey Opiew; their numbers continued to increase. A person named Thatha from the United States sent 60,000 *birrs* to support the group that was left after the death of Chol. On February 9, 2022, Murle attacked people in Gog and Dimma woreda, killing civilians. These attacks were a few of the many attacks that Murle people had against the Anywaa people. Within the same year, many Anywaa people lost their lives, and children were abducted in places like Dimma woreda, Jor woreda, Gog woreda, and they even reached to Abwobo woreda, which is the center of Anywaa lands. During the attack on February 9, 2022, three children were abducted, one person died, and two others were injured. The person who died was on his way from Pinyudo to Teedo kebele riding a motorcycle; he was ambushed and killed by the Murle criminals. When the news reached Gambella, Weny-naam was meeting Ngeeli, and Obang Maak was in Pinyudo. Obang Maak, Weny-naam, Ngeeli, Obang Kut, and their group had to do something. "Why don't we follow them [the Murle] and go wherever that they were heading to and attack them?" said Obang Maak.[8]

Obang Maak, Obang Kut, and the entire group that was created by Chol Okey Opiew started their journey to Pochala, South Sudan. On their way, they killed three honey badgers for food and carried their skins. When they reached Pochala, the king received them and the Anywaa people in Pochala were also getting ready to fight the Murle due to repetitive attacks and abduction of children by the Murle people. When the king asked the group about the food they ate on their long journey, they said, "*Ceye* (plural), *ceri* (singular)," which means "honey badger." So, King Wara-Liek named their group "Lwaa Ceri," which means "clan of honey badgers." This was how the name "Lwaa Ceri" was created. Ngeeli and his team followed and went to Adongo as well. They followed Murle for three days in the forest, and the Murle kept running. According to Ngeeli, the Murle didn't stop and rest at all; they just kept running because they saw the team that was following them.

When they returned from following the Murle people, Ngeeli and his team had a disagreement with the team of Omod Obang (also called Para-naam), who was the head of Anywaa zone militia. Ngeeli Oliru said:

---

8. Interview with Commander Ngeeli Oliru (August 31, 2022).

Lwaa-Ceri

When we came from following the Murle, we went to Gambella town and met with Othow Okoth, Omod Obang, Kwot Agid, and a Nuer security official. Omod Obang said that he chose Obang Kut alone to go with him to follow the Murle. He also complained about a bank account that was opened in the name of Lwaa Ceri for the diaspora to send their support through. Omod Obang wanted the account to be opened in his name or the Anywaa zone administrator name. The leaders in the regional government don't like Kwot and I; they prefer to work with people like Obang Kut.[9]

According to Ngeeli, he and Kwot were denied transportation to join Obang Kut and the Anywaa zone militia after the meeting in Gambella. Obang Kut and the Anywaa zone militia continued the mission by themselves. The group of Lwaa Ceri continued to protect all the Anywaa lands from Murle criminals who always cross the border to Ethiopia and kill people, kidnap children, and destroy property without any response from the government of Ethiopia. Since the creation of Lwaa Ceri, the number of crimes that Murle usually commit in the Anywaa land and the rest of the region drastically dropped, and people started traveling from one place to another without getting killed or kidnapped. Women started collecting cooking wood in the forest again, and children can go to the rivers without any fear. Overall, Lwaa Ceri played a big role in stabilizing the security problem in the border with South Sudan.

---

9. Interview with Commander Ngeeli Oliru (August 31, 2022).

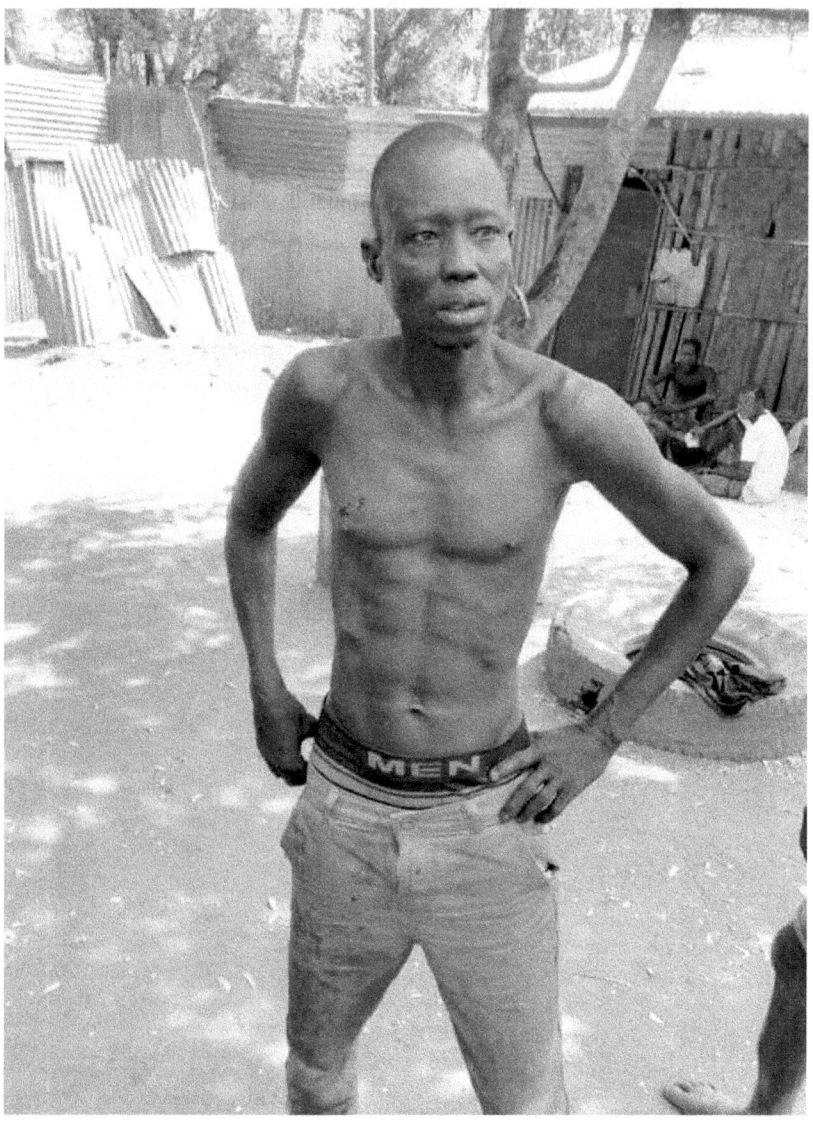

This is Nyikanga Makwach Adhom (an Anywaa), who murdered Chol Okey Opiew on November 24, 2021, in Pinyudo.

Chapter 16

The OLA/F-Shene and GLF attack on Gambella

AFTER ETHIOPIA'S ELECTION IN 2021, there was a Nuer politician, Gatluak Buom, who decided to create a rebel group after losing the election. He named the group the Gambella Liberation Front (GLF), a group made up of all Nuer rebels. This rebel organization collaborated with the TPLF and OLF/A-shene during the two years of war in the northern part of Ethiopia. Their main goal was to destabilize the Gambella region by working with foreign and domestic enemies of the Ethiopian state and overthrow the ruling Prosperity Party. Mr. Thuwat Pal, the uncle of Gatluak Buom Pal, played a diplomacy role with foreign foes of Ethiopia such as Egypt to get military logistics. Gatluak Buom also used the refugee camps in the Gambella region to recruit rebels and started committing atrocities in Gambella town. Before the attack in Gambella town, there were signs that brought a big concern to the residents of Gambella. Two Anywaa boys who were washing in Jabjabe River were shot at by GLF members; one boy was killed, and the other was taken to the hospital. After that, one Anywaa farmer and a boy were killed at night in Angota around the Golli area, and the killers were not found. In the same week, two young men (Anywaa and Amhara young men) were kidnapped by the OLA/F-Shene and GLF terrorists in Aguul-nyaang, and they asked the government for ransom. Everyone in the town became very concerned about the insecurity in Gambella. On June 13, 2022, Kwot Agid and Ngeeli Oliru were invited by Othow Okoth to his office in Gambella town. Othow Okoth was the security affairs officer of

Gambella region. The main reason for the invitation was to inform Ngeeli and Kwot about the possibility of an attack in Gambella by the OLA/F and GLF forces. During the meeting, Ngeeli Oliru responded and said:

> So, now you value us just because the OLA/F and GLF forces are about to attack Gambella town? That is fine, I want you [Othow Okoth and his team] to understand that we cannot let Gambella down and allow some forces to destroy it just because we don't like the leadership. The leaders come and go, but Gambella is our only home, and we will fight and defend it. This is the land we will be buried in. Whether you are in America or anywhere, if you are an Anywaa you will be buried here because this is our ancestral land. Give us ammunition and weapons; we will fight the war.[1]

The people who attended the meeting that night were Bun Wiew (Nuer and the head of militia in Gambella), one security guard of the Ethiopian National Defense Force, Othow Okoth, Ngeeli Oliru, and Kwot Agid. That night, there were names that were given to the regional president Omod Ojulu Obub. Among the lists were the head of the Special Force Commissioner Kong Nyariak (Nuer) and the Police Commissioner Tulit Tut (Nuer). Those two individuals were found to have connections with the GLF and OLA/F, but the president of Gambella took no action.

On June 14, 2022, at approximately 5:30 am, forces belonging to the Oromo Liberation Front (OLF) and Gambella Liberation Front (GLF) launched an attack on Gambella town. The assault continued until 1 p.m. and primarily targeted the Gambella Special Forces stationed in Tier-Jwieni and Don Bosco near Aguul-Nyaang. Aguul-Nyaang is very close to Biher-bireseboch, which is the recent area illegally occupied by Nuer refugees. The GLF forces guided the soldiers from the Oromo Liberation Front/Army (OLF/A) who were armed with machine guns and heavy weapons into the town of Gambella. The gun storage for the special forces and the police was empty, and there was no ammunition in it. Thus, the Gambella Special Forces were caught lacking weapons and ammunition to defend the town, which raised questions about the readiness and preparedness of the special forces to defend and protect the region. It also put the leaders of the special forces and police under suspicion because they had information that the GLF and OLF/A-shene would be attacking the town, and yet they didn't have sufficient preparation. Following a fierce battle, the Gambella Special Forces found themselves outnumbered and subsequently retreated.

1. Interview with Commander Ngeeli Oliru (August 31, 2022).

The OLA/F-Shene and GLF attack on Gambella

This allowed the OLF/A forces, led by GLF Nuer forces, to enter Gambella town through three locations: Addis-sefer, Tier-kidi, and Aguul-nyaang. These areas were mainly targeted by the Oromo and Nuer terrorists because these areas predominantly consisted of Anywaa and Amhara residents. The OLF/A invading army advanced into Tiet-baale (Gonder sefer) near the regional council building and attempted to take over the council building.

During the attack on the town, no gunfire opposing the invasion was observed from the 01 kebele, Cangkwaar (Newland). This 01 kebele, mainly occupied by the Nuer, became a safe haven for the GLF soldiers who escaped the war. The Nuer military leaders who were supposed to be leading, such as Bun Wiew and other generals, went to Newland where there was no sound of guns. Once the OLA/F forces reached the center of the town, they encountered an unexpected response. The Gambella youths joined the fight. This encouraged the fleeing members of the Gambella Special Forces to regroup and fight back, resulting in complete destruction of the OLF terrorists. Those OLF/A soldiers who ventured deeper into the town did not escape alive. The GLF forces, who had been waiting for the OLA/F forces to take control of the city, were forced to flee to Newland after realizing their plans had gone awry. Videos showed them crossing the Jabjabe river, leaving their OLA/F comrades behind while still wearing their uniforms and carrying weapons. "They brought in their OLA/F friends, abandoned them in a vulnerable position, and then fled," stated Dr. Magn Cham, referring to the fleeing GLF forces and the stranded OLF/A forces during his interview with reporter Agwa Gilo on June 25, 2022.

The Gambella Special Forces sealed off all exits in Biher-bireseboch and Addis Sefer, leaving the OLA/F forces with no choice but to seek refuge in residential houses. An Anywaa woman in Tiet-Baale recounted her experience:

> Three OLF forces entered our compound and broke into the house. We were frightened, but they didn't harm me or the children. They simply rummaged through my and my husband's clothes, put them on over their uniforms, and departed.

Knowing that the only way to survive was to blend in the community, OLF forces started entering civilian homes in numerous instances. When they knew that they were discovered, they would start shooting from within these houses. One OLF soldier positioned himself on the roof of a building in Tiet-Baale and fired at the Gambella Special Forces. He was ultimately eliminated by a member of the Gambella Special Forces, who had to enter the building and approach the soldier to neutralize the threat from a closer distance to avoid harming the civilians in the building. The federal forces stationed near the Catholic church remained within their camp throughout the invasion and merely fired shots through their walls to safeguard their own property. At around 10 a.m., federal forces from Gog woreda arrived in Gambella town and joined the fight. At that time, there were only a few OLF forces who were left behind hiding and were still firing shots when they were approached. In the evening, federal commandos arrived in Gambella, but by then, the OLA/F forces had already been defeated. Some OLA/F members remained concealed within the town, while others who managed to escape fled into the surrounding bushes. The commandos assumed control of Gambella town during the night.

On the next day, the bodies of dead OLF forces laid on the streets of Gambella. The prolonged presence of the deceased OLA/F forces' bodies on the streets of Gambella for nearly two days was something that many residents of Gambella complained about. It ignited strong emotions among the Oromo people residing in Gambella and other parts of Ethiopia. Social media such as Facebook was used to post and share the deceased bodies of the OLF/A-shene laying on the streets of Gambella town. Some videos that showed the OLF forces getting killed were also posted and shared on social media, which angered some of the Oromo ethnic group throughout the country. Even though these individuals were OLF forces dressed in military uniforms, Oromo individuals in Gambella were seen gazing at the bodies and shedding tears. Their bitterness and anger stemmed from the realization that these terrorists shared their Oromo ethnicity. Even the perspective of the federal forces seemed to shift, suggesting that the people of Gambella had deliberately targeted and killed Oromo individuals. This highlights the clear presence of colorism in Ethiopia. Whenever a conflict arises between light-skinned individuals and Gambella people, the federal forces are more inclined to take sides. Even in this situation where terrorists were the light-skinned Ethiopians, the federal forces still made it clear that they would have rather seen dead Gambellan civilians on the streets than seeing dead light-skinned terrorists.

For instance, when the federal forces from Gog woreda arrived in Gambella town, the OLF rebels had already been decimated, and their fleeing comrades left the injured ones behind. Near Mikir Bet, an injured OLF soldier had taken cover behind a rock and fired at the special forces. The special forces were deliberating on how to neutralize the threat. Among them, a

The OLA/F-Shene and GLF attack on Gambella

federal soldier wanted to spare the OLF soldier's life. He requested the special forces to wait so he could attempt to convince the rebel to surrender. As he approached the OLF soldier and spoke to him in Afaan Oromo, the rebel shot and killed him. He thought that because they spoke the same language, the OLF terrorist would listen to him and surrender himself. Furthermore, the differing treatment based on skin color becomes apparent when the federal forces appear to prioritize the protection of light-skinned individuals over the dark-skinned people of Gambella. Throughout my upbringing in Gambella, I witnessed numerous cases where in incidents involving a light-skinned person and a dark-skinned person, the light-skinned individual would seek refuge not at the police station but with a federal soldier from the camp near the Catholic church, who were mostly light-skinned Ethiopians. The federal soldier would then proceed to physically assault the dark-skinned person without thoroughly investigating the matter. Whenever a little conflict occurred between light- and the dark-skinned Ethiopians, the light-skinned individual would threaten the dark-skinned Gambellan that they would tell the federal forces. The light-skinned Ethiopians in Gambella viewed the federal forces as their saviors who would side by them against the Gambellans no matter what. The people of Gambella also became aware of the situation, viewing the federal forces as the protectors of the highlanders in Gambella. To this day, the Gambella people still question whether the government of Ethiopia views the dark-skinned Nilotic less Ethiopian compared to the highlanders.

It was anticipated that the Oromo people in Gambella town would be angered following the defeat of the OLF/A rebels (an Oromo ethnic group) by the regional special forces. However, when reports from the Oromo Media Network and Addis Standard media stated that "civilians" had been killed by the Gambella Special Forces, it became evident to the people of Gambella that they were being discriminated against. The Gambella Special Forces had not ventured into the Oromia region or harmed anyone in Gambella town before the OLF invasion. Their actions were devoted to sacrificing their lives to defend the Gambella region and all the ethnic groups it encompasses. Dr. Ojot Miru poignantly questioned, "It is disheartening to hear such reports from the Addis Standard media because who came to attack Gambella? Who were the invaders?" during an interview with reporter Agwa Gilo on June 25, 2022.

Chapter 17

Institutionalized Colorism against Dark-Skinned Gambellans

The Ethiopian Human Rights Commission (EHRC) is an organization based in Addis Ababa, Ethiopia. It was established by the Ethiopian government on July 4, 2000. According to them, their mission is to "promote and ensure the protection of human rights for all." This organization was established to be independent and stands with people whose rights are violated in any part of the regions of Ethiopia. In their core values, they include inclusiveness, which means that the EHRC strives to include a diverse group of people in their leadership and create a team that resembles the diversity in Ethiopia. As an organization that was created to ensure the protection of human rights for all, the EHRC appear to be selective when reporting or condemning human rights abuses happening in Ethiopia under the TPLF government. For instance, the people of Gambella, specifically the Anywaa people, had endured human rights abuses and crimes against humanity under the TPLF government. In 2003, they were brutally massacred by the Ethiopian soldiers and some Highlanders in Gambella. Following the genocide, the Anywaa people faced massive land grabbing, forced displacement, oppression, disappearances, kidnapping, illegal imprisonments, and many other cruel treatments under the government of Ethiopia. Young men were cruelly killed in Gambella prison by the Nuer police and Nuer prisoners, and nobody reported about it. On a normal day when young men were sitting in the Baro-Mado area, the federal forces opened fire at them, killing many of them and wounding some. But the EHRC never reported any of these violations of human rights committed to the Anywaa people.

Prior to the OLF/A-shene and GLF terrorists' invasion in Gambella on June 14, 2022, there were incidents that took place that the EHRC or any Ethiopian news media did not report on. One child was killed and the other wounded by the OLF-shene and GLF in Jabjabe River; two farmers were killed on the farm in Golli (Angota); two young men were kidnapped from a farm and never returned; and one young man from the town was kidnapped and cruelly beaten. Then, the OLF/A-shene and GLF attacked Gambella, but they were defeated. Two days after the OLF/A-shene and GLF invaders were defeated by the Gambella special forces, Gatluak Buom, the chairperson of GLF terrorist organization, initiated a propaganda Facebook campaign, alleging that the Anywaa people had indiscriminately killed Oromo civilians in Gambella town. He proceeded to share a video in which an individual dressed in civilian attire with bound hands was shot by individuals appearing to be in military uniforms. This video quickly went viral and was shared by various OLF and TPLF media outlets. Subsequently, the regional special forces were accused of using excessive force and intentionally targeting Oromo civilians.

While some individuals may have been caught in the crossfire, a common occurrence during intense warfare, the accusation that the Gambella Special Forces deliberately targeted Oromo civilians was false and far from the truth. It is worth noting that the OLA/F terrorist group was responsible for the deaths of at least twenty civilians, including a Canadian citizen named Omod Ojwato, who went unnoticed by the Ethiopian Human Rights Commission (EHRC). This organization's failure to report the people killed or abducted by the OLF/A terrorists before they invaded Gambella raises concerns about how Gambella people are perceived by the EHRC, questioning their recognition as humans or Ethiopians. This is true to almost any organization or institution in Ethiopia. Whether it is a federal government institution or media outlets, they respond differently when something is happening to the dark-skinned Gambella people or those in Benishangul-Gumuz. Which shows the systemic ethnic discrimination and colorism that is embedded in many institutions in Ethiopia.

Colorism played a very big role in the reporting of what happened in Gambella. In the Tier-kidi area, OLF members who were killed were falsely reported as civilians due to their attire consisting of civilian clothing. However, they possessed the same hairstyle commonly associated with

OLF/A terrorists (dreaded hair) and wore their military uniforms underneath the stolen civilian clothes. Furthermore, they neglected to change their military boots, indicating their affiliation. After three days, the Ethiopian Human Rights Commission dispatched representatives to Gambella to gather information regarding the events. They met with local officials and commended the regional special forces for their defense of Gambella and the preservation of civilian lives, preventing a scenario like what occurred to Amhara civilians in Welega, Oromia. Subsequently, they returned to Addis Ababa. During their second visit, they presented a letter indicating that Gambella was among the five regions in Ethiopia where human rights violations had occurred. According to Mr. Ogetu Ading, the Gambella state press secretariat, the regional government provided all the evidence to the EHRC team. However, after receiving the information, the EHRC representatives returned to Addis Ababa and have yet to respond. Days later, they returned for further investigation, but this time, all the investigators were ethnically Oromos. This obviously goes against the core values of the organization which include 'inclusiveness' and strives to ensure diversity in the composition of their leadership and staff. Interestingly, they did not engage with regional officials but exclusively interacted with local Oromo residents in Tiet-Baale, Tier-Kidi, and other Oromo-populated areas in the region. This raised numerous questions about why the EHRC only sent Oromo investigators to exclusively interview Oromo residents in Gambella if they intended to seek the truth. This alone indicates a biased and one-sided report.

In March 2023, Daniel Bekele, the Chief Commissioner of EHRC, and his team visited Gambella with three accusations against the Gambella government. Firstly, they claimed that approximately sixty-three "civilians" were killed by Gambella Special Forces. Secondly, they alleged that numerous "civilians" were injured by the Gambella Special Forces. Lastly, they reported incidents of robberies in Gambella town. Mr. Ogetu Ading provided the following statement:

> Daniel Bekele and his team accused the Gambella Special Forces of killing and injuring civilians and engaging in looting. Consequently, they demanded that the Gambella government hand over the special forces, their leaders, and local youths. Additionally, they requested the government to provide reparations and return

INSTITUTIONALIZED COLORISM

the "civilians'" deceased bodies to their families. Lastly, they expected an apology from the Gambella government.[1]

Upon learning about these demands, Gambella people became angered, leading some young teenagers to vandalize the EHRC sign in Gambella that night. In the eyes of the Gambella people, the EHRC was seen as seeking justice while favoring the OLF/A terrorists solely because of their Oromo ethnic background. After learning about the vandalization of the EHRC sign in Gambella by young teenagers, the EHRC demanded that those who were involved should be held accountable for vandalizing their properties. Mr. Ogetu Ading, the Gambella state press secretariat, made it clear that the government of Gambella would only consider paying reparations or taking any legal action if the EHRC provided the names, kebele, neighborhoods, and families of the alleged "civilians." Mr. Ogetu Ading stated:

> If we do not see the names and addresses of those you claim were "civilians," the government of Gambella will not provide reparations or incarcerate anyone. We know those who came to our region intended to kill us, and our actions were purely in self-defense. It appears that we were expected to be killed without defending ourselves! When the Anywaa people were killed on December 13, 2003, this organization did not demand anything or report on the incident. During Gatluak Tut, federal forces killed children, and the EHRC remained silent. Young individuals were brutally murdered in Gambella Prison as well. Even before the invasion of Gambella, children were killed by the OLF/A and GLF in Jabjabe, two farmers were killed in Golli, and two youths were abducted from an investor's farm, yet the EHRC did not report on any of these incidents. Hence, we conveyed to them that the accusations brought against us following the defeat of OLF/A terrorists were a clear case of discrimination against the Gambella people.[2]

To this day, the EHRC has not released a single name of a "civilian" killed by the Gambella Special Forces. This is because the individuals portrayed as "civilians" by the EHRC were members of the OLF/A terrorists who disguised themselves in civilian attire and attempted to blend in with the community after their defeat. The GLF terrorists survived since they escaped earlier to Newland, where they were hidden by their Nuer people.

---

1. Interview by reporter Agwa Gilo on June 25, 2022.
2. Interview by reporter Agwa Gilo on June 25, 2022.

When the leader of the Gambella Liberation Front (GLF), Gatluak Buom, posted a video on his Facebook account showing people being killed in front of the Gambella Police Station, Mr. Daniel Bekele and his team used the same video as evidence to support their claim that Gambella Special Forces had killed "civilians" based on the individuals appearing to be wearing civilian clothes. However, the EHRC failed to present any further evidence proving that the people in the video were "civilians" beyond their attire. The government of Gambella repeatedly stated that those individuals were OLF/A terrorists who had been captured by the Gambella Special Forces and subsequently taken into custody. Upon reaching the police station, Tulit Tut, the police commissioner, informed the special forces that there was no space for additional prisoners, implying that those in custody should be killed. Consequently, the OLF/A terrorists were executed by orders from Kong Nyariak, the special forces commissioner, and Police Commissioner Tulit Tut. The minister of justice later confirmed this information. According to a report on May 11, 2023, by the Ethiopian National Television, the police commissioner Tulit Tut was heard giving orders in the Nuer language, stating, "Put those highlanders together and kill them all." It was inhumane for these commissioners to issue such orders. However, there was no evidence to suggest that those who were killed were civilians. They were OLF/A soldiers who had changed into civilian clothing, which is a well-known tactic that the OLF mostly use to avoid being caught. The EHRC's narrative of labeling them as "civilians" almost fueled further ethnic conflicts between the Gambella and Oromo people, which was unexpected from organizations of this nature.

There were individuals within the regional government who cooperated with Gatluak Buom, aiming to use the EHRC to portray a negative image of the leadership and the people of Gambella. For instance, during a meeting among regional officials to evaluate the war, Mr. Tut Khor falsely accused the regional special forces of looting, which was precisely what the EHRC later reported. However, the truth is that no looting took place during the war. There were no incidents of bank robberies or theft of private property. On the contrary, the special forces acted to prevent the looting the OLF/A insurgents would have carried out. When the OLF/A terrorists take control of an area, one of the things that they usually do is break into banks and rob shops and private properties. This was prevented by the Gambella special forces in Gambella town, and the people of Gambella expressed their gratitude by standing on the side of the special forces despite the accusations by the EHRC.

Gambella has always been a place that welcomes people from all backgrounds. It is a region known for its diverse ethnic groups, representing almost all of Ethiopia. The Oromo people have peacefully coexisted with the Gambella community for centuries, engaging in trade, intermarriage and contributing to the region's development, just like any other Ethiopians. The strong sense of community in Gambella means that if someone goes missing or passes away, it quickly becomes known throughout the town. Similarly, the arrival of a new face in the neighborhood doesn't go unnoticed. Given this closeness and interconnectedness, the people of Gambella urged Mr. Daniel Bekele and the EHRC organization to cease demonizing both the Gambella community and the special forces, who have made sacrifices to protect the region. The people of Gambella, specifically the Anywaa, accused the EHRC of unjustly targeting the special forces as criminals and viewed the report as a retaliation by the Oromo leaders in power due to the ethnicity of the deceased OLF/A soldiers. They also strongly condemn these accusations and view them as discriminatory, despite the fact that the actions of the special forces were in self-defense.

The Anywaa Plea for Justice, Accountability, and Intervention by the International Community

Justice has never been served for the victims of the Anywaa genocide in 2003. The Anywaa people have continued to suffer in the refugee camps in South Sudan, Kenya, and Uganda. Those who refused to leave their ancestral land in Gambella are on the verge of extinction due to the ongoing silent genocide, insecurities, and constant killing and displacement by the South Sudanese refugees. If the international community does not respond to save this small ethnic group that is facing existential threat from both the Ethiopia state and South Sudan, the Anywaa people will go extinct. It is a full responsibility of the international community and the United Nations (UN) to intervene and prevent any acts of systemic or active ethnic cleansing by any country or government. The government of Ethiopia led by the TPLF organization is responsible for the Anywaa genocide in 2003 and responsible for the continued crimes against humanity committed following the genocide. The individuals who planned and carried out the Anywaa genocide were Meles Zenawi, Addisu Legesse, Bereket Simon,

Samora Yunis, Yohannes Gebremeskel, Abadula Gemeda, Abay Tsehaye, Dr. Gebre-Aba Barnabas, Almaw Alemeraw, Sibhat Nega, Tadesse Haile-Selase, Omod Obang Olom, Tsegaye Beyene, and Shambel Amare.[3] None of those individuals faced justice for their involvement in carrying out the Anywaa genocide and the crimes against humanity to the minority Anywaa population. The TPLF organization must pay reparations to the victims' families for the genocide, torture, illegal detentions, land grabbing, crimes against humanity, and generational trauma that they have caused to the Anywaa people under their government.

The EPRDF government led by the TPLF political party committed acts against the civilian Anywaa population which constitute crimes against humanity and are punishable as violations of customary international law. Based on the report by Genocide Watch and Survivor's Rights International on February 25, 2004, the government of Ethiopia under TPLF committed the following crimes against humanity to the Anywaa people on December 13, 2003:

1. Widespread and systematic murders and executions of Anuaks.
2. Arson and murder to forcibly deport the Anuak population.
3. Mass rape of Anuak women and girls.
4. Forced pregnancy to produce non-Anuak children.
5. Enforced disappearances of Anuak persons.
6. Arbitrary arrests, detention, and torture of Anuak persons.
7. Purposeful transmission of HIV/AIDS to Anuak rape victims (inhumane acts).
8. Intentional mutilation of Anuak persons.
9. Other cruel or inhumane acts intentionally causing great suffering or bodily harm.[4]

The following acts committed by the EPRDF led by the TPLF political organization constitute acts of genocide according to Genocide Watch and Survivor's Rights International:

---

3. Reported by the former president of Gambella, Mr. Okello Akway.
4. *"Today is the Day of Killing Anuaks."*

1. The intentional killing of members of the Anuak ethnic group, targeted solely because they are Anuak, destroying a substantial part of the Anuak group.
2. The deliberate targeting of members of the Anuak ethnic group to cause serious bodily or mental harm.
3. The deliberate infliction on the Anuak group, through burning of homes and destruction of food supplies, of conditions of life calculated to bring about its physical destruction.
4. The systematic use of rape as a weapon against a large number of Anuak women in order to destroy the Anuak ethnic group, by forcing Anuak women to bear the children of non-Anuak fathers, intentional infection of Anuak women with HIV/AIDS so as to cause future death, and rapes of Anuak young girls so as to prevent them from having children in the future.[5]

As it is concluded by Genocide Watch and Survivors' Rights International that what happened to the Anywaa people on December 13, 2003, was an act of genocide and constituted crimes against humanity, all the individuals and organizations who were involved should be held accountable under the violation of international law by which Ethiopia is bound. Ethiopia should cease its silent and active genocide activities to wipe out the Anywaa Luo Ethiopians from their lands.

The plea and demand of the Anywaa people is not just for the Ethiopian state to cease its systemic genocide toward the Anywaa community but also for the international community to hear the voice of these diminishing human beings intentionally getting wiped out by the government of Ethiopia. The Anywaa people are pleading to the United Nations and the international community to intervene and prevent them from the threat of extinction that they are facing under the Ethiopian state. Like everybody else, the Anywaa people have the right to exist on their ancestral lands without being targeted or oppressed. The natural resources in Anywaa lands should not be a reason for their extinction. The Anywaa are raising their voice of desperation and crying out to the international community to hear them. Just like Jessen stated in 1904—that the Anywaa people are like "flying fish"—I would argue that Anywaa people today are like fish on dry land gasping for oxygen and exposed to all kinds of predators. When

---

5. *"Today is the Day of Killing Anuaks."*

the Anywaa are targeted and killed by the Murle and Nuer from South Sudan in the territory of Ethiopia, the government of Ethiopia turns a blind eye because it satisfies their interest. The government does not provide them basic human necessities because it is in the interest of the Ethiopian state to have no Anywaa tribe in Gambella in the coming years. The Anywaa are slowly dying and disappearing from the face of the earth with or without the knowledge of the international community due to their small population and confined voice.

Addressing Institutionalized Colorism and Discrimination in Ethiopia

The colorism and discrimination against dark-skinned people in Ethiopia is systematic and institutionalized. Gambella and Benishangul-Gumuz are the poorest and the most marginalized regions in Ethiopia. Gambella and Benishangul-Gumuz are mostly inhabited by the Nilotic people, and there are highlander settlers who were brought to these regions by the Derg government. Today, there are many highlanders who immigrated to these regions and became residents. The land grabbing and forced displacement of the Nilotics in these places by the government and highlanders have been taking place since the Derg government. Consequently, there have been conflicts and disputes taking place between the Nilotic and the highlanders in both Gambella and Benishangul-Gumuz over the lands. The encroachment and land grabbing by the highlanders threatened the Nilotic peoples indigenous in these places. Furthermore, being minorities compared to the light-skinned Ethiopians and the lack of representation of the Nilotic peoples created a lack of trust among the people. The discrimination and colorism are just adding to the existing mistrust that was already created during slavery and the expansion of the Ethiopian state.

Even though the dark-skinned Nilotic people are constitutionally acknowledged as Ethiopians, they are not treated equally like the rest of light-skinned Ethiopians (highlanders). The massive influx of highlanders into Gambella, and the occupation of the land have threatened the indigenous people of Gambella and impacted their way of life. When a highlander goes to Gambella, they will be given a local ID and allowed to own lands and properties. But dark-skinned Gambellans cannot be allowed to have a local ID card in any other places in Ethiopia except in Gambella. They cannot own lands anywhere else but Gambella. Even when a Gambellan

INSTITUTIONALIZED COLORISM

gives birth to a child in Addis Ababa, the child will not be issued a birth certificate in Addis Ababa. They must go back to Gambella and get a birth certificate from Gambella. It is also very hard for a Gambellan to acquire an ID card in Addis Ababa compared to a highlander even though they meet all the requirements. This is an institutional discrimination against the dark-skinned Ethiopians in their country. Gambella is known for its fertile soil and natural resources. However, when a local Gambellan tries to loan money from the banks for investments, they are more likely to be denied compared to the highlanders. Thus, the majority of investors and business owners in Gambella become predominantly the highlanders.

The Gambella people are also underrepresented at the federal government level and in Ethiopian media outlets. There has not been a Gambellan appointed as one of the council of ministers in Ethiopia since the Derg government. When Dr. Abiy Ahmed came to power, the people of Gambella anticipated that he might have a diverse council of ministers from all the regions. However, he only appointed half women and half men; none of them were Gambellans or Nilotic. Even though he was applauded for appointing half of the council of ministers with women ministers, the exclusion of Nilotic people pointed to the role of colorism in the federal government. Dark-skinned Ethiopians are somehow viewed as less competent even for the jobs within their regions. For instance, Gambella hosts the largest population of refugees in Ethiopia, and many NGOs are present in the region. But when it comes to hiring for the jobs available at these NGOs, the people of Gambella are also underrepresented in these organizations. That is because the NGOs in Gambella tend to hire people from other regions and Addis Ababa and bring them to Gambella even though there are a big number of unemployed, well-educated Gambellans. The majority of investors and those who are working for the NGOs in Gambella are the highlanders. As a result, when there is an open position in any of these organizations in Gambella, HR (usually highlanders) would be more likely to hire a highlander than a Gambellan. There are many occasions where I was asked where I was from. But whenever I replied that I was from Ethiopia, I would receive a response like "you don't look Ethiopian!" This is something that the Nilotic Ethiopians deal with, which raises a question about what face of Ethiopians that Ethiopia shows the world. There are more than eighty ethnic groups living in Ethiopia, and the lack of representation of the majority of these groups at the national level and the media outlets gives the world a different perspective about the diverse groups in Ethiopia.

Anywaa | Part 4

The Original Local Names of the Neighborhoods in Gambella Town

The names of most neighborhoods in Gambella town were changed in the last three to four years, mostly by the highlanders who are residing in the areas. The Anywaa people who inhabited the areas before the Nuer refugees and highlanders settled in Gambella had names for the neighborhoods and places that were originally used. Most of the names had historical meaning, while others were named after incidents or physical marks. Here is the list of the neighborhood names that were changed by the highlanders and the Nuer:

1. Abwobobeer (also known as Thuur Odii) was changed to Selam Sefer, which is an Amharic word which literally translates to "neighborhood of peace."
2. Agulnyaang was changed to Ye-leboch Sefer, which is an Amharic word which literally translates to "the neighborhood of thieves."
3. Ajala gaala was changed to Gebiya, which literally means "market."
4. Cangkwaar was changed to Newland by the Nuer refugee students who were brought to Gambella and sponsored by the UN.
5. Gamnyikwacgilo or Omiininga was changed to Bure Sefer because most of the highlanders in the area are from Bure in western Ethiopia.
6. Gog bajomi (also known as Tietkaak) was changed to Metu Mazuria.
7. Lo Oloni (also known as Ye-cwaay or Kumbooni) was changed to Ayertena, which is also an Amharic word.
8. Owalinga was changed to Care Gebiya.
9. Pwol jaay was changed to Shiro Meda.
10. Achiil was changed to Homtu Jirtu, which is an Oromo name meaning "nothing present."
11. Tiercwaa was changed to Kulubi.
12. Tietbaale was changed to Gonder Sefer because the highlanders that resided in the area were mostly from Gonder in the Amhara region.
13. Tierjwieni was changed to Addis Sefer, which is an Amharic word literally meaning "new neighborhood" in English.

Institutionalized Colorism

14. Tierkidi was changed to Wollo Sefer because most of the highlanders that settled in the area are mainly from Wollo in the northern part of Ethiopia.
15. Wangjwiel was changed to Abwobo Mazuria.
16. Wangjwieni was changed to Sellase because of a new church that was built in the area named Sellase.
17. Wi pwoljaay was changed to 8100.
18. Ya-chiil was changed to Michael Sefer, named after a new Orthodox church that was opened in the area.

Glossary

Abudho: The royal bead for the Anywaa chiefs.

Achota (Olangngo): An alcoholic beverage that the Anywaa make using corn flour mixed with yeast.

Adïma: An Anywaa word that literally means "oppression."

Afegubaye Adarash: The House of Speakers meeting room or hall.

Agazi Commandos: A special group of forces that were named after one of the TPLF Agazi (Zeru) Gessesse. They are loyal to the TPLF regime, and they were well-trained to encounter any threat to the TPLF government.

Agwaga song: One of the oldest traditional Anywaa types of songs.

Ajiba (pl. Ajiibe): The name that Anywaa people use to call Murle or Beir. They are Surmic-speaking and part of the Nilotic group. They are mainly found in Jonglei state in South Sudan.

Ajwiel (pl. Ajwieli): An Anywaa word to refer to the Dinkas. Dinkas are a tribe that is mainly found in South Sudan.

Alem Bekagn: An Amharic phrase that means "I am done with the world."

Anya Nya I: Also spelled "Anyanya I." It is a separatist movement that was formed by the Southern Sudanese and fought against the Sudanese government during the first civil war in Sudan from 1955 to 1972.

Araki: A strong alcoholic beverage that was introduced to the Anywaa people by the settlers who were brought to Gambella by the Derg regime.

Atham-gaala: Tobacco that the Anywaa people received from the gaala or the Oromos.

Glossary

Bajaj: A three-wheeler mainly manufactured in India. It is used as a means of transportation in many cities of Ethiopia.

Balabat: An Amharic word that was traditionally used to refer to the social status of wealthy and landowners in society.

Baqo Zabana: Guards of the lowlands.

Bariya: An Amharic word that literally means "slave."

Baro-Mado: A general Amharic word that is used to refer to the other side of the Openo River. The Anywaa people called it "Loo Olooni Looga."

Berbere spice: An Ethiopian spice blend made with chili peppers and other ingredients.

Biel: An arranged marriage where a young girl or adult woman is forced into a marriage with some one in exchange for Dimuuye.

Biher-bireseboch: An Amharic word that is literally translated as "nations and nationalities." In 2015, the tenth Ethiopian Nations, Nationalities and People's Day was celebrated in Gambella. Each of the five ethnic groups in Gambella were given lands in Gambella town as most of them came from the countryside to celebrate. After the celebration finished, they left those areas and went back to their places. However, the Nuer refused to go back, and they forcefully settled in the area.

Bimm: The tax collector for the king.

Birhaneselam: An Amharic word meaning "the light of peace."

Boordhi or Abaara: An alcoholic beverage that is made with unleavened cooked corn flour and then mixed with yeast.

Cheway or Cwaay: An Anywaa word that literally means "creator." The Anywaa believe that the first chief to govern the Anywaa people was named Cwaay.

Congress Party: This was a political party that was created by the Anywaa elites when the GPLP and GPDUP were merged to form the GPDF in 1998.

Deeloneen Pergambella: This is a Facebook account that was created and run by an unknown group of people. It played a big role in exposing the corruption and maladministration in Gambella, which led to the expulsion of Gatluak Tut and Senay Akwor from their position in 2018.

Glossary

Dha-Anywaa: The language that Anywaa people speak. It is sometimes written as Anuak.

Dhaldiim: An Anywaa word that literally means "defying or resisting oppression."

Dhi-øt Nyec: The royal clan.

Dhøk-uudï: An Anywaa word for the sub-clan. The Anywaa people have twelve sub-clans, and they are distinguished by a unique name: *loe*. Each subclan has their own unique *loe*.

Dimuuy (Dimui) (pl. Dimuuye): A blue glass bead; it is a very important and special bead for the Anywaa people. The Anywaa use it for the bride price (dowry) and for compensation.

Ethiopic Fidel: The Amharic alphabet, which comes from the Ge'ez script (Fidel).

Fasika (Fasica): One of the most important holidays for the Ethiopian Orthodox Tewahedo Church in Ethiopia. It is an Amharic, Ge'ez, and Tigrayan word for Easter.

Federal Guday Ministry: Ministry of Federal Affairs.

Fetha Nagast: The law of the kings.

Fitawrari: An Ethiopian military title for the commander of the vanguard.

Gaala: The name that the Anywaa use to refer to the Oromo or any highlanders (Amhara, Tigrayan).

Gada system: Also spelled "Gadaa." A governance system that is traditionally used by the Oromo people.

Gallas: A derogatory Amharic word that was used to refer to the Oromo as slaves.

Gillo: An Anywaa word that is used to refer to any disease that causes the stomach or abdomen to swell or get larger. The name Gilo comes from the word Gillo.

Gimmira: An Amharic word for "taxes" or "tribute."

Ginbar Party: Literally means Front Party. The Woyane or TPLF used the term Ginbar Party to describe their party.

Goma: An Amharic word for a tire (rubber wheel).

Glossary

Jo-kwori: It is a phrase that the Anywaa people use to refer to criminals who murder people. It literally translates as "people who committed homicide." Jo-kwori are known for kidnapping children and using them as bait for lions and tigers.

Jur (pl. Juure): An Anywaa word for "foreigners."

Jwok (pl. Juu): An Anywaa word for "God" or "gods."

Jwok-Nyingolabwuo: The Anywaa name for the good God.

Jwok-Nyoodungo: The Anywaa name for the bad and evil god.

Kade: A traditional Anywaa practice of tattooing or marking the skin. It was viewed by the Anywaa people as a sign of beauty.

Kar Wang: The security advisor to the headman or kwaaro.

Katha-Radhi/Kwach-Lwaak: The general chief of staff in the Anywaa kingdom.

Kebele: An Amharic word for "wards."

Keew: The Anywaa word for "borders."

Keewa: An Anywaa food made of corn flour and mixed with groundnuts.

Keseli: An Amharic word for "coal."

Khat: A stimulant plant that is widely consumed in East African countries, Southern Africa, and the Arabian Peninsula. Its leaves are chewed for the stimulant effects it provides.

Kunyjuur (Kugnjuur): A form of magic which the Anywaa believed can prevent you from getting hit by a bullet during the fight and makes your enemies go to sleep when you are present. The Anywaa also believe that *Kunyjuur* can use nature such as strong wind or rains against the enemy.

Kwaac Kodo: The drum beater or whistle-blower in the palace of the Anywaa king.

Kwaaro (pl. Kwaari) or Rwoth: This means "chief." The Anywaa use *kwaaro* to call or address anyone who holds any kind of leadership position.

Kwar: This means "headmanship." The Anywaa people use *kwar* for any kind of leadership as well.

Glossary

Kwon (quon): A traditional Anywaa food made with corn flour. It is called *ogali* in some African countries, and it can be eaten by dipping it in any kind of stew.

Langngo: An Anywaa word for "slave."

Lwaa Ceri: A group or clan of honey badgers.

Lwaak-gan-duong: The special forces of the Anywaa kingdom.

Lwaak Mar Kaadi: Military intelligence in the Anywaa kingdom.

Lwaak-Nga-Apeiya: All royal guards in the Anywaa kingdom.

Mee: The king's maternal uncles.

Mender: An Amharic word for "village."

Mengist state: This means the state of the government.

Mikir Bet: The council building.

Naak: The removal of lower front teeth. In Anywaa culture, women removed their lower front teeth during their adolescence; it was considered a sign of beauty.

Naath: Another name for the Nuer tribe.

Nyec: Kingship.

Nyeya (pl. Nyeye): It is an Anywaa word that literally means king. It is sometimes spelled *Nyiya*.

Nyiatwiel: The minister of interior and public relations in the Anywaa kingdom. Nyiatwiel can be also literally translated as "angel."

Nyiatwiel mar Bat-Boogi: Deputy.

Nyibaatbogo: The social secretary and servant to the headman or *kwaaro*.

Nyibur: The Anywaa word for a leadership position that is equivalent to that of prime minister.

Nyikeeno: The food service affairs in the palace of the Anywaa king.

Nyikugo: In the Anywaa kingdom, Nyikugo is the king's deputy. It can be also used to refer to a messenger or a prophet.

Nyipem: The Anywaa word for a prince.

Nyithengo: The deputy of Nyikugo.

Nywaak: An Anywaa word that literally means "sharing" in English.

Glossary

Ocwok (Uchuok): The royal bead for the Anywaa kings.

Ogooli: An alcoholic drink made with honey and a tree that the Anywaa call *agiima*.

Olum neger wede thor ginbar: Literally translated as "all and everything to the war front."

Otak: is a practice in which two hardwoods are used to trap and squash the legs between them. It was used for punishment, especially during a marriage. For instance, when a man impregnates a woman and he denies it, he would be punished by *otak*.

Qenyazmach: An Ethiopian military title for the commander of the right wing.

Shaleqa: An Amharic word for the commander of a thousand.

Shambel: An Ethiopian military title for the commander of two hundred fifty.

Shanqella: is a derogatory Amharic word that was used to refer to the Nilotic or dark-skinned people in Ethiopia (mostly people from Gambella and Benishangul-Gumuz).

Shifta: An Amharic word for a rebel or bandit.

Therfi shi-aleka: The EPRDF compound in Gambella town.

Wachatha: An alcoholic beverage made with honey and yeast.

Week Ngoomo: Dha-Anywaa. Can literally be translated as "owners of the land."

Wenbede: An Amharic word that means "bandit."

Woreda: An Amharic word for "district."

Yet'abatachew: An Amharic insult, similar to saying that "they deserve this s-word."

Interviewees

1. Mr. Awinya Nyegilo Ojaay was interviewed on October 2, 2023
2. Commander Bare Agid was interviewed on August 30, 2022
3. Commander Ngeeli Oliru was interviewed on August 31, 2022
4. Dr. Magn Ochala Cham (Ph.D) was interviewed on September 25, 2023
5. Former President of Gambella Mr. Okello Akway was interviewed on August 29, 2022
6. Former President of ACANA Mr. Oron Ochala was interviewed on April 26, 2022
7. Community elder Mr. Willie Gilo Lumson was interviewed on January 18, 2021.
8. Interview by reporter Agwa Gilo on June 25, 2022.

References

Agula, Bogale Aligaiz. "Interaction and Conflict among the Nuer and Anuak Communities in the Gambella Region, Southwest Ethiopia." *American Journal of History and Culture* 3.16 (2020) 1–7.
"Anuak Displacement and Ethiopian Resettlement." Cultural Survival, Feb 24, 2010. https://www.culturalsurvival.org/publications/cultural-survival-quarterly/anuak-displacement-and-ethiopian-resettlement.
Bayissa, Regasa. "The Derg-SPLM/A Cooperation: An Aspect of Ethio-Sudan Proxy Wars." *Ethiopian Journal of the Social Sciences and Humanities* 5.2 (2011) 19–44. https://doi.org/10.4314/ejossah.v5i2.63648.
Campbell, Gwyn, et al. *Women and Slavery*. Athens, OH: Ohio University Press, 2007.
Cascão, Ana Elisa. "Resource-based Conflict in South Sudan and Gambella (Ethiopia): When Water, Land and Oil Mix with Politics." https://repositorio.iscte-iul.pt/bitstream/10071/5111/1/10Ana_Casca%cc%830_Resource.pdf.
Cham, Magn. "Ethiopia's EPDRF and the Massacre of Anyuaks in December 2003." *Sudan Tribune*, Aug 3, 2006. https://sudantribune.com/article17425.
Chavkin, Sasha. "New Evidence Ties World Bank to Human Rights Abuses in Ethiopia." International Consortium of Investigative Journalists, Apr 16, 2015. https://www.icij.org/investigations/world-bank/new-evidence-ties-world-bank-human-rights-abuses-ethiopia.
Cliffe, Lionel, and Basil Davidson. *The Long Struggle of Eritrea for Independence and Constructive Peace*. Trenton, NJ: Red Sea, 1988.
———. "Power and Its Discontents: Anywaa's Reactions to the Expansion of the Ethiopian State: 1950–1991." *International Journal of African Historical Studies* 48.1 (2015) 31–49.
Collins, Robert. "Civil Wars in the Sudan." *History Compass* 5.6 (2007) 1778–805. https://doi.org/10.1111/j.1478-0542.2007.00473.x.
Evans-Pritchard, Edward E. *The Political System of the Anuak of the Anglo-Egyptian Sudan*. New York: AMS, 1977.
Feyissa, Dereje. "The Experience of the Gambella Regional State." In *Ethnic Federalism: The Ethiopian Experience in Comparative Perspective*, edited by David Turton, 208–30. Athens, OH: Ohio University Press, 2006.
———. *Playing Different Games: The Paradox of Anywaa and Nuer Identification Strategies in the Gambella Region, Ethiopia*. New York: Berghahn, 2011.

References

"Former President Says Indifference by Regime Encourages Cross Border Raid." Ethiopian Satellite Television and Radio, Mar 22, 2017. https://ethsat.com/2017/03/gambella-former-president-says-indifference-regime-encourages-cross-border-raid.

Gebeyehu, Temesgen. "Ethnic Conflict, Interaction and Cohabitation in Africa: The Case of Nuer and Anuak." *Eastern Africa Social Science Research Review* 29.2 (2013) 97–112. https://doi.org/10.1353/eas.2013.0008.

Geertz, Clifford. "Works and Lives: The Anthropologist as Author." Stanford, CA: Stanford University Press, 1988.

"A History of the Translation of the Anywaa's Bible, Wëël Jwøk." *Gambella Star News*, Nov 15, 2015. https://www.gambellastarnews.com/index.php/more/topic/536-a-history-of-the-translation-of-the-anyuak-bible.

Horne, Felix. "Waiting Here for Death." Jan 16, 2012, Human Rights Watch. https://www.hrw.org/report/2012/01/17/waiting-here-death/forced-displacement-and-villagization-ethiopias-gambella.

Hulne, Rocky. "Leaving a Mark: Austin Man Was Highly Involved in the Community." *Austin Daily Herald*, Dec 1, 2021. https://www.austindailyherald.com/2021/11/leaving-a-mark-austin-man-was-highly-involved-in-the-community.

Iadarola, Antoinette. "Ethiopia's Admission into the League of Nations: An Assessment of Motives." *International Journal of African Historical Studies* 8.4 (1975) 601–22. https://doi.org/10.2307/216698.

Jessen, B. H. "South-western Abyssinia." *Geographical Journal* 25.2 (1905) 62–163.

Kibret, G. D., et al. "Trends and Spatial Distributions of HIV Prevalence in Ethiopia." *Infectious Diseases of Poverty* 8.1 (2019) 158–71. https://doi.org/10.2307/1775880.

Kurimoto, Eisei. "Multidimensional Impact of Refugees and Settlers in the Gambela Region, Western Ethiopia." Kyoto: Kyoto University Press, 2005.

———. "Natives and Outsiders: The Historical Experience of the Anywaa of Western Ethiopia." *Journal of Asian and African Studies* 43 (1992) 1–43. https://www.ethiopia-insight.com/wp-content/uploads/2021/05/Kurimoto.pdf.

Kuyok, Kuyok Abol. *South Sudan: The Notable Firsts*. Bloomington IN: AuthorHouse, 2015.

Markakis, John. *Ethiopia: The Last Two Frontiers*. Woodbridge, UK: James Currey, 2011.

"Mission." Oromo Liberation Front. http://oromoliberationfront.org/english/mission/.

Muhumad, Abdirahman Ahmed, and Mohamed A. Siraj. "Somali Region in Ethiopia: Historical Developments during the Period 1884–1995." *Academic Journal for Somali Studies* 2 (2017) 60–75. https://www.researchgate.net/publication/340630138_Somali_Region_in_Ethiopia_Historical_Developments_during_the_Period_1884–1995.

Opap, O. O. *Unsung Giants: Who Fought to Keep Africa Free*. Osborne Park, Australia: Africa World Books, 2020.

"Over 60 Killed in Attacks on 19 Locations Displacing over 8,000 people." July 7, 2002. Prevent Genocide International. http://www.preventgenocide.org/africa/ethiopia/gambella/2003.htm.

Pankhurst, Richard. "The Ethiopian Slave Trade in the Nineteenth and Early Twentieth Centuries: A Statistical Inquiry." *Journal of Semitic Studies* 9.1 (1964) 220–28. https://doi.org/10.1093/jss/9.1.220.

Partee, Charles. *Adventure in Africa: The Story of Don McClure: From Khartoum to Addis Ababa in Five Decades*. Grand Rapids: Zondervan, 1992.

Perner, Conradin.

Perner, Conradin. *Living on Earth in the Sky: The Anyuak: An Analytic Account of the History and the Culture of a Nilotic People*. Basel: Helbing & Lichtenhahn, 2014.

References

———. *Why Did You Come If You Leave Again?: The Narrative of an Ethnographer's Footprints among the Anyuak in South Sudan*. Bloomington, IN: Xlibris, 2017.

"Today is the Day of Killing Anuaks": Crimes Against Humanity, Acts of Genocide and Ongoing Atrocities Against the Anuak People of Southwestern Ethiopia. Genocide Watch, Feb 25, 2004. http://www.genocide-watch.com/images/CampaignDoc_Today_is_the_Day_of_Killing_Anuaks.pdf.

Zewde, Bahru. *Society, State, and Identity in African History*. Bamako, Mali: Forum For Social Studies, 2008.

———. "Relations between Ethiopia and the Sudan on the Western Ethiopian Frontier 1898–1935" (PhD diss., University of London, 1976).

www.ingramcontent.com/pod-product-compliance
Lightning Source LLC
Chambersburg PA
CBHW072130160426
43197CB00012B/2052